I0505850

The MSP Cybersecurity Survival Guide

Your Step-By-Step Guide to Spot Social Engineering and Phishing, Stop Ransomware and Fraud, and Sleep Soundly at Night

Acknowledgements

I'd like to thank my wonderful, insightful, and loving wife, Safiya, for teaching me her incredible gift of unending empathy and love.

I'd like to thank my siblings, Cassidy, Kinzey, and Boden, for their warmth, love, and infinite assistance through a tumultuous upbringing.

I'd also like to thank my mentors and role models in software, security and business, John Shedd, Joseph Brunsman, Brian Kurtz, Donald Spann, Craig Simpson, Michael Crist, Aaron Ross, Robert Herjavec, Stu Sjouwerman, Peter Bauer, Holden Fenner, Andrew Long, Adam Tischler, Brian Krebs, Reid Hoffman, Alex Berman, Conor McCluskey, Brian Halligan, Adam

Tischler, Mansur Habib, Chip Justice, NR Narayana Murthy and Michael Echols for their guidance, criticism, and encouragement.

And my late parents, Sherri Lynn Jackson and Michael Andrew McHale, for giving everything they ever had and more to give our family a fighting chance here in the United States.

Table of Contents

What is Cybersecurity?

What are the risks to having poor cybersecurity?

What can you do to improve your cybersecurity?

Hacker, attacker, or intruder.

Malicious code

Vulnerabilities

Good Security Habits

How can you minimize the access others have to your information?

Improve password security.

Create a strong password.

Consider using a password manager.

Use two-factor authentication, if available.

Use security questions properly.

Create unique accounts for each user per device.

Choose secure networks.

Keep all of your personal electronic device software current.

Be suspicious of unexpected emails.

Cybersecurity for Electronic Devices

Why does cybersecurity extend beyond computers?

What types of electronics are vulnerable?

First, Remember physical security.

Second, Keep software up to date.

Third, Use strong passwords.

Fourth, Disable remote connectivity.

Fifth, Encrypt files.

Finally, Be cautious of public Wi-Fi networks.

How Do I Improve the Security of Internet-Enabled Devices?

Evaluate your security settings.

Ensure you have up-to-date software.

Connect carefully.

Use strong passwords.

Protecting Your Privacy

How do you know if your privacy is being protected?

Read the Privacy policy

Look for Evidence that your information is being encrypted

Do business with credible companies

Do not use your primary email address in online submissions

Avoid submitting credit card information online

How can you protect yourself?

Research your investment opportunities.

Be wary of online information.

Check privacy policies.

Conduct transactions on devices you control.

Make sure that your transactions are encrypted.

Verify that the website is legitimate.

Monitor your investments.

Use strong passwords.

Use and maintain anti-virus software.

Use anti-spyware tools.

Keep software up to date.

Evaluate your security settings.

Avoiding Copyright Infringement

Email programs offer many "user-friendly" features.

What steps can you take to protect yourself and others in your address book?

Be wary of unsolicited attachments, even from people you know.

Keep software up to date.

Trust your instincts.

Save and scan any attachments before opening them.

Turn off the option to automatically download attachments.

Consider creating separate accounts on your computer.

Apply additional security practices.

Reducing Spam

What is spam?

How can you reduce the amount of spam?

Be careful about releasing your email address.

Check privacy policies.

Be aware of options selected by default.

Use filters or spam tagging.

Report messages as spam.

Don't follow links in spam messages.

Disable the automatic downloading of graphics in HTML mail.

Consider opening an additional email account.

Use privacy settings on social networking sites

Don't spam other people

Benefits of BCC

What is BCC?

Why would you want to use BCC?

Run a full scan on your computer with your antivirus software

Run a legitimate product specifically designed to remove spyware

Make sure that your anti-virus and anti-spyware software are compatible

Protecting Against Malicious Code

What is malicious code?

How can you protect yourself against malicious code?

Install and maintain antivirus software.

Use caution with links and attachments.

Block pop-up advertisements.

Use an account with limited permissions.

Disable external media AutoRun and AutoPlay features.

Change your passwords.

Keep software updated.

Back up data.

Install or enable a firewall.

Use anti-spyware tools.

Monitor accounts.

Avoid using public Wi-Fi.

What do you need to know about antivirus software?

Automatic scans

Manual scans

Investigate your options in advance.

Limit the number of programs you install.

How do you recover if you become a victim of malicious code?

Minimize the damage.

Remove the malicious code.

Social Engineering

Using Instant Messaging and Chat Rooms
Safely

What are the differences between some of
the tools used for real-time communication?

Chat rooms

Bots

What are the dangers?

How can you use these tools safely?

Evaluate your security settings.

Make sure to disable automatic
downloads.

Be conscious of what information you
reveal.

Try to verify the identity of the person you
are talking to, if it matters.

Don't believe everything you read.

Keep software up to date.

Real-World Warnings Keep You Safe Online

Why are these warnings important?

What are some warnings to remember?

Don't trust candy from strangers.

If it sounds too good to be true, it probably is.

Don't advertise that you are away from home

Lock up your valuables

Have a backup plan

Keeping Children Safe Online

What unique risks are associated with children?

What can you do?

Be involved

Keep your computer in an open area

Set rules and warn about dangers

Monitor computer activity

Keep lines of communication open

Consider partitioning your computer into separate accounts

Consider implementing parental controls

Dealing with Cyber Bullies

What is cyberbullying?

Why has cyberbullying become such a problem?

How can you protect yourself or your children?

Teach your children good online habits.

Keep lines of communication open.

Watch for warning signs.

Limit availability of personal information.

Avoid escalating the situation.

Document the activity.

Use and maintain security software, and keep all software up to date.

Do not plug an unknown USB drive into your computer.

Disable Autorun.

Data Leakages

Safeguarding Your Data

Why isn't "more" better?

How can you protect both your personal and work-related data?

Use and maintain anti-virus software and a firewall

Regularly scan your computer for spyware

Keep software up to date

Evaluate your software's settings

Avoid unused software programs

Consider creating separate user accounts

Establish guidelines for computer use

Use passwords and encrypt sensitive files

Follow corporate policies for handling and storing work-related information

Dispose of sensitive information properly

Follow good security habits

Proper Disposal of Electronic Devices

Why is it important to dispose of electronic devices safely?

Computers, smartphones, and tablets

Digital media

External hardware and peripheral devices

Gaming consoles

What are some effective methods for removing data from your device?

Backing up data.

Deleting data.

Visit www.HailBytes.com for free cybersecurity resources!

Computers.

Smartphones and tablets.

Digital cameras, media players, and
gaming consoles.

Office equipment (e.g., copiers, printers,
fax machines, multifunction devices).

Overwriting.

Destroying.

Magnetic media degaussers.

Solid-state destruction.

CD and DVD destruction.

How can you safely dispose of out-of-date
electronic devices?

Effectively Erasing Files

Where do deleted files go?

What are the risks?

Can you erase files by reformatting?

What additional levels of security are available?

Something you know.

Something you have.

Something you are.

What other measures keep your passwords secure?

"Salt and hash" passwords.

Use strong authentication recovery mechanisms.

Implement an account lockout policy.

Set accounts to automatically disable.

What if you lose your password or certificate?

Safe Browsing

How Anonymous Are You?

What information is collected?

IP address

Limit the amount of personal information you post.

Remember that the internet is a public resource.

Be wary of strangers.

Be skeptical.

Evaluate your settings.

Be wary of third-party applications.

Use strong passwords.

Check privacy policies.

Keep software, particularly your web browser, up to date.

Use and maintain anti-virus software

Shopping Safely Online

Why do online shoppers have to take special precautions?

How do attackers target online shoppers?

What is crypto mining?

What is cryptojacking?

What types of systems and devices are at risk for cryptojacking?

    Computer systems and network devices

    Mobile devices

    Internet of Things devices

How do you defend against cryptojacking?

    Use and maintain antivirus software.

    Keep software and operating systems up-to-date.

    Use strong passwords.

    Change default usernames and passwords.

    Check system privilege policies.

    Apply application whitelisting.

Be wary of downloading files from websites.

Recognize normal CPU activity and monitor for abnormal activity.

Disable unnecessary services.

Uninstall unused software.

Validate input.

Install a firewall.

Create and monitor blacklists.

Mobile Devices & Traveling

Protecting Your Portable Device: Physical Security

What is at risk?

How can you protect your laptop or internet-enabled device?

Password-protect your computer

Keep your valuables with you at all times

Other Products and Programs by David McHale

Monthly Phishing Simulations

On-Demand Phishing Servers

Basic Security Awareness Training Platform

Advanced Security Awareness Training Platform

Written Information Security Program - Digital +
Hardcover, with Annual Reprints

National Institute Of Standards and Technology
Cyber Security Framework Audit

Written Information Security Policies - Digital +
Hardcover, with Annual Reprints

Book David McHale To Speak!

Introduction to The MSP Cybersecurity Survival Guide

Dear Friend,

Welcome to The MSP Cybersecurity Survival Guide.

This represents nearly 10 years of hard work, experience and the efforts of my incredible team and customers. Maybe you're one of them!

I wanted to take a moment to share some thoughts with you in no particular order about what to expect in this book.

If you have a short attention span, have ADD (like me), or learn better and faster with video, make sure to head over to hailbytes.teachable.com because you can join our training platform that explains the principles in this book in a concise video format.

First, it's interactive. There are lots of opportunities for you to go deeper in the content, gain access to free training videos, participate in some interactive masterclass events and more.

Second, this book is for business. It's intended to help you grow your security culture, protect your business, and sleep easier at night. It isn't intended to serve poets, fiction-writers or people who want to write memoirs, children's books or novels - however , it will work for those businesses but I don't focus on them.

Third, it's for implementers. You'll see there's LOTS of ideas that you can use to secure any business type. If you're the type who's looking for free, easy security, this isn't the book for you. I'm not here to blow smoke up your butt and lie to you.

Fourth, this book wasn't intended to be a NY Times #1 Bestseller. It's designed to start a conversation with you, give us a chance to get to know each other better, develop trust, a bond and ultimately help us decide if we will work together someday.

Fifth, this is a book that's packed with content and lots of ideas. It's a WHAT book, as well as a WHY and step-by-step HOW TO book. My intention and the purpose of this book is to show you the most powerful ways to protect yourself, expose you to multiple ways to defend yourself against criminals, build a security culture, gain insight and leverage the latest technology and strategies available and set yourself up for long-term growth and peace of mind in the future. We have a how-to system available that includes everything you need to execute what you read in these pages.

I'll be the first to admit, I'm a shameless self-promoter - and I want to help you protect more people, keep your business making money and add value to your life and everyone you come in contact with. You'll notice there are opportunities throughout this book to register and watch videos and YES, I do have some great products I'd like to sell to you because they work and you'll have a better life with them.

Having said that, if you like what you read, or most of what you read, I'd absolutely, positively love to hear from you and get to know you better and find out what you learned - or better yet post a picture or video on my facebook page at www.facebook.com/hailbytes or tweet me @hailbytes.

The BEST way to start a relationship with me will be to visit www.HailBytes.com/common-cybersecurity-questions, watch my free Q&A session, and learn more about how to protect your business and brand. I'm looking forward to getting to know you better!

Sincerely,
David McHale in Laurel, MD USA

PS - I wrote and edited this book myself. There are probably some spelling, grammatical and layout errors. If you find one, will you do me a favor and tell me what you find by sending me an email to david@hailbytes.com? Just note the section, sentence and mistake and I'll fix it right away *and thank you for your help.* I'm all about results, implementation and speed and chose to give you tools that keep you safer over perfection and procrastination.

PPS - if you love this, will you please post a review on Amazon at https://www.amazon.com/dp/B085M21G7W? If you DON'T like it, send me an email, tell me why and I'll give you your money back, ok? My direct email is david@hailbytes.com

Please be kind. I have two kids. They read what people say about me online and so do their friends. There's no sense in dragging two innocent kids into something unnecessary. Nobody likes a bully and our world has too much hate in it the way it is. Let's be friends. Cool?

Welcome to the book!

My name's David McHale.

I'm a professional security consultant that's helped people from dozens of organizations learn how to better protect themselves from the growing threat of cybercrime.

Some of the organizations that have trusted me to help them in recent years include the Department of Transportation, the Federal Aviation Administration, the Federal Highway Administration, and the Department of the Interior.

It is becoming increasingly important for organizations to develop a culture that prioritizes cyber security.

The training and security implementation are no longer solely IT or security team functions.

They are now functions for everyone.

It's important for each and every one of us to learn how to better protect ourselves, our families, and our employers.

Why group it all together like that?

It's because professional and personal lives are being melded together more often than not.

Not to mention your behaviors are very similar in what you do, in that which you do at home is what you'll most likely do at work.

You're constantly hearing warnings about new threats, new breaches, and new attacks. It can be overwhelming to keep up with.

When you or your business does fall victim to an attack, people want to point fingers.

That is never the right way to approach security.

I want you to know that as we go through this course together I'll speak to you from a place of compassion and not of condescension.

I don't want to beat you over the head or speak down to you.

My number one goal is to help you understand how to protect yourself.

And we'll do that by going over what threats are important to know about, why they're important to understand, and what they look like in real life.

So now you might be wondering, "why is this a big deal?"

91% of cyber attacks start with someone just like you or me clicking on something we think is trustworthy, and being taken advantage of to get access to our company's network.

The average cost of an attack like that succeeding is $5 million dollars according to the NCSA.

This means there is a huge need to protect devices.

Both in your home and in your workplace.

Your nerdy friend or your IT department can't fully protect you anymore.

It's extremely important to understand:

All of us have an important role to play in security, no matter what level you're at.

And I get it, there's hacks and intrusions and technical stuff that you can't help detect and stop.

I'm not asking you to learn complicated hacking skills that require the kind of experience that's taken me years to build up.

In all honesty an attacker is 16.6x more likely to breach your company by taking advantage of your trust by way of a phishing email than with any fancy attack.

This is effective because you're busy juggling a hundred different things at your job.

You want to work quickly, and keep your organization moving forward, so it's easy to fall prey to these kinds of attacks if you don't know exactly what to look for.

By investing this time in developing your security awareness, you're potentially saving your company millions of dollars in damage from cyber crime.

I saw a story recently about a cosmetics company that suffered a ransomware attack that came through a phishing email and the hackers wound up accidentally deleting the files they'd held ransom.

The entire company of 50 people was wiped out overnight because they weren't keeping backups and someone happened to open a file from a phishing email.

As you go through this course, please don't hesitate to reach out and ask me any questions you have.

This course is intended to be a living reference for you to come back and review every few months.

And remember...

Security awareness is just as important for Mac users too.

Don't buy into the myth that you're safe because you don't use Windows.

Usernames and passwords from your banking website or retirement account or insurance company will work on any computer regardless of the operating system.

Plus, there are plenty of viruses made specifically for Mac.

What is Cybersecurity?

Defending yourself against cyberattacks starts with understanding the risks associated with cyber activity, what some of the basic cybersecurity terms mean, and what you can do to protect yourself.

It seems that everything relies on computers and the internet now.

Communication like email, and smartphones.

Entertainment like digital cable, and mp3s.

Transportation like car engine systems, and airplane navigation.

Shopping like online shopping, and credit cards.

Medicine like medical equipment, and medical records...

And the list goes on.

How much of your daily life relies on computers?

How much of your personal information is stored either on your own computer or on someone else's system?

Cybersecurity involves protecting that information by preventing, detecting, and responding to cyber attacks.

What are the risks to having poor cybersecurity?

There are many risks, some more serious than others.

Among these dangers are malware erasing your entire system…

An attacker breaking into your system and altering files,

an attacker using your computer to attack others,

or an attacker stealing your credit card information and making unauthorized purchases.

Unfortunately, there's no 100 percent guarantee that even with the best precautions some of these things won't happen to you, but there are steps you can take to minimize the chances.

What can you do to improve your cybersecurity?

Heed credible security warnings and move quickly to fix them.

When vulnerabilities come to your attention, listen carefully and then get a move on. In the HTC America case, the FTC charged that the company didn't have a process for receiving and addressing reports about security vulnerabilities. HTC's alleged delay in responding to warnings meant that the vulnerabilities found their way onto even more devices across multiple operating system versions. Sometimes, companies receive security alerts, but they get lost in the shuffle. In Fandango, for example, the company relied on its general customer service system to respond to warnings about security risks. According to the complaint, when a researched contacted the business about a vulnerability, the system incorrectly categorized the report as a password reset request, sent an automated response, and marked the message as "Resolved" without flagging it for further review, As a result, Fandango didn't learn about the vulnerability until FTC staff contacted the company. The lesson for other businesses? Have an effective process in place to receive and address security vulnerability reports. Consider a clearly publicized and effective channel (for example, a dedicated email address like security@yourcompany.com) for receiving reports and flagging them for your security staff.

The first step in protecting yourself is to recognize the risks and become familiar with some of the terminology associated with them.

Hacker, attacker, or intruder.

These terms are applied to the people who seek to exploit weaknesses in software and computer systems for their own gain.

Although their intentions are sometimes fairly benign and motivated solely by curiosity, their actions are typically in violation of the intended use of the systems they are exploiting.

The results can range from mere mischief like creating a virus with no intentionally negative impact to

---

malicious activity such as stealing or altering information.

Malicious code

Malicious code, also called malware, is a broad category that includes any code that could be used to attack your computer.

Malware can have the following characteristics:

It might require you to actually do something before it infects your computer.

This action could be opening an email attachment or going to a particular webpage.

Some forms of malware propagate without user intervention and typically start by exploiting a software vulnerability.

Once the victim computer has been infected, the malware will attempt to find and infect other computers.

This malware can also propagate via email, websites, or network-based software.

Some malware claims to be one thing, while in fact doing something different behind the scenes.

For example, a program that claims it will speed up your computer may actually be sending confidential information to a remote intruder.

Examples of malware include: viruses, worms, and ransomware.

Vulnerabilities

Vulnerabilities can be caused by software programming errors.

Attackers may try to take advantage of these errors to infect your computer, so it is important to apply updates or patches that address known vulnerabilities.

I'll cover this more in our "Understanding Patches" module.

Good Security Habits

Use industry-tested and accepted methods.

When considering what technical standards to follow, keep in mind that experts already may have developed effective standards that can apply to your business. Savvy companies don't start from scratch when it isn't necessary. Instead, they take advantage of that collected wisdom. The ValueClick case illustrates that principle. According to the FTC, the company stored sensitive customer information collected through its e-commerce sites in a database that used a non-standard ,proprietary form of encryption. Unlike widely-accepted encryption algorithms that are extensively tested, the complaint charged that ValueClick's method used a simple alphabetic substitution system subject to significant vulnerabilities. The company could have avoided those weaknesses by using tried-and-true industry-tested and accepted methods for securing data.

Let's go over a few Good Security Habits to help you stay safe.

There are some simple habits you can adopt that, if performed consistently, will dramatically reduce the chances that the information on your computer will be lost or corrupted.

How can you minimize the access others have to your information?

It may be easy to identify people who could gain physical access to your devices.

Family members, roommates, coworkers, people nearby, and others.

Identifying the people who have the capability to gain remote access to your devices is not as simple.

As long as your device is connected to the internet, you are at risk for someone accessing your information.

However, you can significantly reduce your risk by developing habits that make it more difficult.

Improve password security.

Passwords continue to be one of the most vulnerable cyber defenses.

Create a strong password.

Use a strong password that is unique for each device or account.

Longer passwords are more secure.

An option to help you create a long password is using a passphrase.

Visit www.HailBytes.com for free cybersecurity resources!

Four or more random words grouped together and used as a password.

To create strong passwords, the National Institute of Standards and Technology (NIST) suggests using simple, long, and memorable passwords or passphrases.

Consider using a password manager.

Password manager applications manage different accounts and passwords while having added benefits, including identifying weak or repeated passwords.

There are many different options, so start by looking for an application that has a large install base so 1 million users or more and an overall positive review, more than 4 stars.

Properly using one of these password managers will help improve your overall password security.

Use two-factor authentication, if available.

Two-factor authentication is a more secure method of authorizing access.

It requires two out of the following three types of credentials:

something you know like a password or PIN, something you have like a token or ID card, and something you are like a biometric fingerprint.

Because one of the two required credentials requires physical presence, this step makes it more difficult for a threat actor to compromise your device.

Use security questions properly.

For accounts that ask you to set up one or more password reset questions, use private information about yourself that only you would know.

Answers that can be found on your social media or facts everyone knows about you can make it easier for someone to guess your password.

Create unique accounts for each user per device.

Set up individual accounts that allow only the access and permissions needed by each user.

When you need to grant daily use accounts administrative permissions, do so only temporarily.

This precaution reduces the impact of poor choices, such as clicking on phishing emails or visiting malicious websites.

Choose secure networks.

Use internet connections you trust, such as your home service or Long-Term Evolution or LTE connection through your wireless carrier.

Public networks are not very secure, which makes it easy for others to intercept your data.

If you choose to connect to open networks, consider using antivirus and firewall software on your device.

Another way you can help secure your mobile data is by using a Virtual Private Network service.

This allows you to connect to the internet securely by keeping your exchanges private while you use Wi-Fi.

When setting up your home wireless network, use WPA2 encryption.

All other wireless encryption methods are outdated and more vulnerable to exploitation.

In early 2018, the Wi-Fi Alliance announced WPA3 as a replacement to the longstanding WPA2 wireless encryption standard.

As WPA3-certified devices become available, users should employ the new standard.

Keep all of your personal electronic device software current.

Manufacturers issue updates as they discover vulnerabilities in their products.

Automatic updates make this easier for many devices.

Including computers, phones, tablets, and other smart devices.

But you may need to manually update other devices.

Only apply updates from manufacturer websites and built-in application stores.

Third-party sites and applications are unreliable and can result in an infected device.

When shopping for new connected devices, consider the brand's consistency in providing regular support updates.

Be suspicious of unexpected emails.

Phishing emails are currently one of the most prevalent risks to the average user.

The goal of a phishing email is to gain information about you, steal money from you, or install malware on your device.

Be suspicious of all unexpected emails.

I'll cover this in more depth in our "Avoiding Social Engineering and Phishing Attacks" module.

Cybersecurity for Electronic Devices

Protect devices that process personal information

Securing information stored on your network won't protect your customers if the data has already been stolen through the device that collects it. In the 2007 Dollar Tree investigation, FTC staff said that the business's PIN entry devices were vulnerable to tampering and theft. As a result, unauthorized persons could capture consumer's payment card data, including the magnetic stripe data and PIN, through an attack known as "PED Skimming." Given the novelty of this type of attack at the time, and a number of other factors, staff closed the investigation. However, attacks targeting point-of-sale devices are now common and well-known, and businesses should take reasonable steps to protect such devices from compromise.

Next we'll talk about Cybersecurity for Electronic Devices.

When you think about cybersecurity, remember that electronics such as smartphones and other Internet-enabled devices may also be vulnerable to attack.

Take appropriate precautions to limit your risk.

Why does cybersecurity extend beyond computers?

Actually, the issue is not that cybersecurity extends beyond computers.

It's that computers extend beyond traditional laptops and desktops.

Many electronic devices are computers.

From cell phones and tablets to video games and car navigation systems.

While computers provide increased features and functionality, they also introduce new risks.

Attackers may be able to take advantage of these technological advancements to target devices previously considered "safe."

For example, an attacker may be able to infect your cell phone with a virus, steal your phone or wireless service, or access the data on your device.

Not only do these activities have implications for your personal information, but they could also have serious consequences if you store corporate information on the device.

What types of electronics are vulnerable?

Any piece of electronic equipment that uses some kind of computerized component is vulnerable to software imperfections and vulnerabilities.

The risks increase if the device is connected to the internet or a network that an attacker may be able to access.

Remember that a wireless connection also introduces these risks.

The outside connection provides a way for an attacker to send information to or extract information from your device.

Let's talk about a few ways you can protect yourself:

First, Remember physical security.

Having physical access to a device makes it easier for an attacker to extract or corrupt information.

Do not leave your device unattended in public or easily accessible areas.

Second, Keep software up to date.

If the vendor releases updates for the software operating your device, install them as soon as possible.

Installing them will prevent attackers from being able to take advantage of known problems or vulnerabilities.

Third, Use strong passwords.

Choose devices that allow you to protect your information with passwords.

Select passwords that will be difficult for thieves to guess, and use different passwords for different programs and devices.

Do not choose options that allow your computer to remember your passwords.

Fourth, Disable remote connectivity.

Some mobile devices are equipped with wireless technologies, such as Bluetooth, that can be used to connect to other devices or computers.

You should disable these features when they are not in use.

Fifth, Encrypt files.

If you are storing personal or corporate information, see if your device offers the option to encrypt the files.

By encrypting files, you ensure that unauthorized people can't view data even if they can physically access it.

When you use encryption, it is important to remember your passwords and passphrases; if you forget or lose them, you may lose your data.

Finally, Be cautious of public Wi-Fi networks.

Follow these recommendations when connecting to any public wireless hotspot like on an airplane or in an airport, hotel, train/bus station or café:

Confirm the name of the network and exact login procedures with appropriate staff to ensure that the network is legitimate.

Do not conduct sensitive activities, such as online shopping, banking, or sensitive work, using a public wireless network.

Only use sites that begin with "https://" when online shopping or banking.

Using your mobile network connection is generally more secure than using a public wireless network.

Debunking Some Common Myths

Verify Compliance.

Security can't be a "take our word for it" thing. Including security expectations in contracts with service providers is an important first step, but it's also important to build oversight into the process. The Upromise case illustrates that point. There, the company hired a service provider to develop a browser toolbar. Upromise claimed that the toolbar, which collected consumer's browsing information to provide personalized offers, would use a filter to "remove any personally identifiable information" before transmission. But, according to the FTC, Upromise failed to verify that the service provider had implemented the information collection program in a manner consistent with Upromises' privacy and security policies and the terms in the contract designed to protect consumer information. As a result, the toolbar collected sensitive personal information - including financial

account numbers and security codes from secure web pages
- and transmitted it in clear text. How could the company
have reduced that risk? By asking questions and following
up with the service provider during the development process.

Let's take a minute before we move on to debunk some
common myths about cyber security.

How are these myths established?

There's no one cause for these myths.

They may have been formed because of a lack of
information, an assumption, knowledge of a specific
case that was then generalized, or some other source.

As with any myth, they are passed from one individual
to another, usually because they seem legitimate
enough to be true.

Why is it important to know the truth?

While believing these myths may not present a direct
threat, they may cause you to be more lax about your
security habits.

If you are not diligent about protecting yourself, you may be more likely to become a victim of an attack.

So let's go over some common myths and what the truth is behind them:

Myth #1: Anti-virus software and firewalls are 100% effective.

Truth: Anti-virus software and firewalls are important elements to protecting your information.

However, neither of these elements are guaranteed to protect you from an attack.

Combining these technologies with good security habits is the best way to reduce your risk.

We'll cover both of these in more depth in Understanding Anti-Virus Software and Understanding Firewalls later on in the course.

Myth #2: Once software is installed on your computer, you do not have to worry about it anymore.

Truth: Vendors may release updated versions of software to address problems or fix vulnerabilities.

We'll cover this process in Understanding Patches later on.

You should install the updates as soon as possible.

Some software even offers the option to obtain updates automatically.

Making sure that you have the latest virus definitions for your anti-virus software is especially important.

Myth #3: There is nothing important on your machine, so you do not need to protect it.

Truth: Your opinion about what is important may differ from an attacker's opinion.

If you have personal or financial data on your computer, attackers may be able to collect it and use it for their own financial gain.

Even if you do not store that kind of information on your computer, an attacker who can gain control of your computer may be able to use it in attacks against other people.

You'll learn more about these kinds of attacks in our "Understanding Denial-of-Service Attacks" module and our "Understanding Hidden Threats: Rootkits and Botnets" modules later on in the book.

Myth #4: Attackers only target people with money.

Truth: Anyone can become a victim of identity theft.

Attackers look for the biggest reward for the least amount of effort, so they typically target databases that store information about many people.

If your information happens to be in the database, it could be collected and used for malicious purposes.

It is important to pay attention to your credit information so that you can minimize any potential damage.

You'll learn more about this in our "Preventing and Responding to Identity Theft" module later on in the course.

Myth #5: When computers slow down, it means that they are old and should be replaced.

Truth: It is possible that running newer or larger software programs on an older computer could lead to slow performance...

but you may just need to replace or upgrade a particular component like the memory, operating system, CD or DVD drive, etc..

Another possibility is that there are other processes or programs running in the background.

If your computer has suddenly become slower, it may be compromised by malware or spyware, or you may be experiencing a denial-of-service attack.

You'll learn more about this in our Recognizing and Avoiding Spyware module and our Understanding Denial-of-Service Attacks module.

It's time to build your security culture anytime, anywhere, on any device. Not only do you get the tools and systems to become one of the most well-defended managed service providers around, you learn the mindset it takes to become successful in cybersecurity and can pass both on to your clients.

You'll also learn more about how you can assess, educate, and monitor your staff. There are hundreds of ways to improve your security based on your unique business. Now is the time to become competition and recession-proof.

Visit www.HailBytes.com for free security resources!

User & Device Accountability

Securing the Internet of Things

Let's talk briefly about Securing the Internet of Things

The Internet of Things is becoming an important part of everyday life.

Being aware of the associated risks is a key part of keeping your information and devices secure.

The Internet of Things refers to any object or device that sends and receives data automatically through the Internet.

This rapidly expanding set of "things" includes tags.

These are also known as labels or chips that automatically track objects.

It also includes sensors, and devices that interact with people and share information machine to machine.

Why Should We Care?

Cars, appliances, wearables, lighting, healthcare, and home security all contain sensing devices that can talk to other machines and trigger additional actions.

Examples include devices that direct your car to an open spot in a parking lot;

mechanisms that control energy use in your home;

control systems that deliver water and power to your workplace;

and other tools that track your eating, sleeping, and exercise habits.

This technology provides a level of convenience to our lives, but it requires that we share more information than ever.

The security of this information, and the security of these devices, is not always guaranteed.

What Are the Risks?

Though many security and resilience risks are not new, the scale of interconnectedness created by the Internet of Things increases the consequences of known risks and creates new ones.

Attackers take advantage of this scale to infect large segments of devices at a time, allowing them access to the data on those devices or to, as part of a botnet, attack other computers or devices for malicious intent.

How Do I Improve the Security of Internet-Enabled Devices?

Ensure Proper Configuration.

Encryption - even strong methods - won't protect your users if you don't configure it properly. That's one message businesses can take from the FTC's actions against Fandango and Credit Karma. In those cases, the FTC alleged that the companies used SSL encryption in their mobile apps, but turned off a critical process known as SSL certificate validation without implementing other compensating security measures. THat made the apps vulnerable to man-in-the-middle attacks, which could allow hackers to decrypt sensitive information the apps transmitted. Those risks could have been prevented if the companies' implementations of SSL had been properly configured.

Without a doubt, the Internet of Things makes our lives easier and has many benefits; but we can only reap these benefits if our Internet-enabled devices are secure and trusted.

The following are important steps you should consider to make your Internet of Things more secure.

Evaluate your security settings.

Most devices offer a variety of features that you can tailor to meet your needs and requirements.

Enabling certain features to increase convenience or functionality may leave you more vulnerable to being attacked.

It is important to examine the settings, particularly security settings, and select options that meet your needs without putting you at increased risk.

If you install a patch or a new version of software, or if you become aware of something that might affect your device, reevaluate your settings to make sure they are still appropriate.

Ensure you have up-to-date software.

When manufacturers become aware of vulnerabilities in their products, they often issue patches to fix the problem.

Patches are software updates that fix a particular issue or vulnerability within your device's software.

Make sure to apply relevant patches as soon as possible to protect your devices.

Connect carefully.

Once your device is connected to the Internet, it's also connected to millions of other computers, which could allow attackers access to your device.

Consider whether continuous connectivity to the Internet is needed.

Use strong passwords.

Passwords are a common form of authentication and are often the only barrier between you and your personal information.

Some Internet-enabled devices are configured with default passwords to simplify setup.

These default passwords are easily found online, so they don't provide any protection.

Choose strong passwords to help secure your device.

So now you've learned the basics of securing the internet of things.

Protecting Your Privacy

Let's talk about Protecting Your Privacy.

Before submitting your email address or other personal information online, you need to be sure that the privacy of that information will be protected.

To protect your identity and prevent an attacker from easily accessing additional information about you, be cautious about providing your birth date, Social Security number, or other personal information online.

How do you know if your privacy is being protected?

Read the Privacy policy

Before submitting your name, email address, or other personal information on a website, look for the site's privacy policy.

This policy should state how the information will be used and whether or not the information will be distributed to other organizations.

Companies sometimes share information with partner vendors who offer related products or may offer options to subscribe to particular mailing lists.

Look for indications that you are being added to mailing lists by default—failing to deselect those options may lead to unwanted spam.

If you cannot find a privacy policy on a website, consider contacting the company to inquire about the policy before you submit personal information, or find an alternate site.

Privacy policies sometimes change, so you may want to review them periodically.

Look for Evidence that your information is being encrypted

To prevent attackers from stealing your personal information, online submissions should be encrypted so that it can only be read by the appropriate recipient.

Many sites use Secure Sockets Layer (SSL) or Hypertext Transport Protocol Secure (https).

A lock icon in the bottom right corner of the window indicates that your information will be encrypted.

Some sites also indicate whether the data is encrypted when it is stored.

If data is encrypted in transit but stored insecurely, an attacker who is able to break into the vendor's system could access your personal information.

What additional steps can you take to protect your privacy?

Do business with credible companies

Before supplying any information online, consider the answers to the following questions:

Do you trust the business?

Is it an established organization with a credible reputation?

Does the information on the site suggest that there is a concern for the privacy of user information?

Is legitimate contact information provided?

If you answered "No" to any of these questions, avoid doing business online with these companies.

Do not use your primary email address in online submissions

Submitting your email address could result in spam.

If you do not want your primary email account flooded with unwanted messages, consider opening an additional email account for use online.

Make sure to log in to the account on a regular basis in case the vendor sends information about changes to policies.

Avoid submitting credit card information online

Some companies offer a phone number you can use to provide your credit card information.

Although this does not guarantee that the information will not be compromised, it eliminates the possibility that attackers will be able to hijack it during the submission process.

Devote one credit card to online purchases

To minimize the potential damage of an attacker gaining access to your credit card information, consider opening a credit card account for use only online.

Keep a minimum credit line on the account to limit the amount of charges an attacker can accumulate.

Avoid using debit cards for online purchases

Credit cards usually offer some protection against identity theft and may limit the monetary amount you will be responsible for paying.

Debit cards, however, do not offer that protection.

Because the charges are immediately deducted from your account, an attacker who obtains your account information may empty your bank account before you even realize it.

Take advantage of options to limit exposure of private information

Default options on certain websites may be chosen for convenience, not for security.

For example, avoid allowing a website to remember your password.

If your password is stored, your profile and any account information you have provided on that site is readily available if an attacker gains access to your computer.

Also, evaluate your settings on websites used for social networking.

The nature of those sites is to share information, but you can restrict access to limit who can see what.

Now you understand the basics of protecting your privacy.

If you'd like to learn much more, come join my complete security awareness course and I'll teach you everything you need to know about staying safe online.

Understanding Voice over Internet Protocol (VoIP)

Let's spend the next few minutes Understanding Voice over Internet Protocol or VoIP.

With the introduction of VoIP, you can use the Internet to make telephone calls instead of relying on a separate telephone line.

However, the technology does present security risks.

What is voice over Internet protocol (VoIP)?

Voice over Internet protocol (VoIP), also known as IP telephony, allows you to use your Internet connection to make telephone calls.

Instead of relying on an analog line like traditional telephones, VoIP uses digital technology and requires a high-speed broadband connection such as DSL or cable.

There are a variety of providers who offer VoIP, and they offer different services.

The most common application of VoIP for personal or home use is Internet-based phone services that rely on a telephone switch.

With this application, you will still have a phone number, will still dial phone numbers, and will usually have an adapter that allows you to use a regular telephone.

The person you are calling will not likely notice a difference from a traditional phone call.

Some service providers also offer the ability to use your VoIP adapter any place you have a high-speed Internet connection, allowing you to take it with you when you travel.

What are the security implications of VoIP?

Because VoIP relies on your Internet connection, it may be vulnerable to many of the same problems that face your computer and even some that are specific to VoIP technology.

Attackers may be able to perform activities such as intercepting your communications, eavesdropping, taking control of your phone, making fraudulent calls from your account, conducting effective phishing attacks by manipulating your caller ID, and causing your service to crash.

Activities that consume a large amount of network resources, like large file downloads, online gaming, and streaming multimedia, may affect your VoIP service.

There are also inherent problems to routing your telephone over your broadband connection.

Unlike traditional telephone lines, which operate despite an electrical outage, if you lose power, your VoIP may be unavailable.

VoIP services may also introduce problems for location-dependent systems such as home security systems or emergency numbers such as 911.

How can you protect yourself?

Keep software up to date.

If the vendor releases updates for the software operating your device, install them as soon as possible.

Installing them will prevent attackers from being able to take advantage of known problems or vulnerabilities.

Use and maintain anti-virus software.

Anti-virus software recognizes and protects your computer against most known viruses.

However, attackers are continually writing new viruses, so it is important to keep your antivirus software current.

Take advantage of security options.

Some service providers may offer encryption as one of their services.

If you are concerned about privacy and confidentiality, you may want to consider this and other available options.

Install or enable a firewall.

Firewalls may be able to prevent some types of infection by blocking malicious traffic before it can enter your computer.

Some operating systems actually include a firewall, but you need to make sure it is enabled.

Evaluate your security settings.

Both your computer and your VoIP equipment or software offer a variety of features that you can tailor to meet your needs and requirements.

However, enabling certain features may leave you more vulnerable to being attacked, so disable any unnecessary features.

Examine your settings, particularly the security settings, and select options that meet your needs without putting you at increased risk.

Now you understand the basics of VoIP.

Understanding Bluetooth Technology

Many electronic devices are now incorporating Bluetooth technology to allow wireless communication with other Bluetooth devices.

Before using Bluetooth, it is important to understand what it is, what security risks it presents, and how to protect yourself.

What is Bluetooth?

Bluetooth is a technology that allows devices to communicate with each other without cables or wires.

It is an electronics "standard," which means that manufacturers that want to include this feature have to incorporate specific requirements into their electronic devices.

These specifications ensure that the devices can recognize and interact with other devices that use Bluetooth technology.

Many popular manufacturers are making devices that use Bluetooth technology.

These devices include mobile phones, computers, and personal digital assistants or PDAs.

The Bluetooth technology relies on short-range radio frequency, and any device that incorporates the technology can communicate as long as it is within the required distance.

The technology is often used to allow two different types of devices to communicate with each other.

For example, you may be able to operate your computer with a wireless keyboard, use a wireless headset to talk on your mobile phone, or add an appointment to your friend's PDA calendar from your own PDA.

What are some security concerns?

Depending upon how it is configured, Bluetooth technology can be fairly secure.

You can take advantage of its use of key authentication and encryption.

Unfortunately, many Bluetooth devices rely on short numeric PIN numbers instead of more secure passwords or passphrases.

If someone can "discover" your Bluetooth device, he or she may be able to send you unsolicited messages or abuse your Bluetooth service, which could cause you to be charged extra fees.

Worse, an attacker may be able to find a way to access or corrupt your data.

One example of this type of activity is "bluesnarfing," which refers to attackers using a Bluetooth connection to steal information off of your Bluetooth device.

Also, viruses or other malicious code can take advantage of Bluetooth technology to infect other devices. If you are infected, your data may be corrupted, compromised, stolen, or lost.

You should also be aware of attempts to convince you to send information to someone you do not trust over a Bluetooth connection.

How can you protect yourself?

Disable Bluetooth when you are not using it

Unless you are actively transferring information from one device to another, disable the technology to prevent unauthorized people from accessing it.

Use Bluetooth in "hidden" mode

When you do have Bluetooth enabled, make sure it is "hidden," not "discoverable."

The hidden mode prevents other Bluetooth devices from recognizing your device.

This does not prevent you from using your Bluetooth devices together.

You can "pair" devices so that they can find each other even if they are in hidden mode.

Although the devices, for example, a mobile phone and a headset, will need to be in discoverable mode to initially locate each other, once they are "paired" they will always recognize each other without needing to rediscover the connection.

Be careful where you use Bluetooth

Be aware of your environment when pairing devices or operating in discoverable mode.

For example, if you are in a public wireless "hotspot," there is a greater risk that someone else may be able to intercept the connection than if you are in your home or your car.

Evaluate your security settings

Most devices offer a variety of features that you can tailor to meet your needs and requirements.

However, enabling certain features may leave you more vulnerable to being attacked, so disable any unnecessary features or Bluetooth connections.

Examine your settings, particularly the security settings, and select options that meet your needs without putting you at increased risk.

Make sure that all of your Bluetooth connections are configured to require a secure connection.

Take advantage of security options

Learn what security options your Bluetooth device offers, and take advantage of features like authentication and encryption.

Understanding Denial-of-Service Attacks

You may have heard of denial-of-service attacks launched against websites, but you can also be a victim of these attacks.

Denial-of-service attacks can be difficult to distinguish from common network activity, but there are some indications that an attack is in progress.

What is a denial-of-service (DoS) attack?

A denial-of-service (DoS) attack occurs when legitimate users are unable to access information systems, devices, or other network resources due to the actions of a malicious cyber threat actor.

Services affected may include email, websites, online accounts like banking, or other services that rely on the affected computer or network.

A denial-of-service is accomplished by flooding the targeted host or network with traffic until the target cannot respond or simply crashes, preventing access for legitimate users.

DoS attacks can cost an organization both time and money while their resources and services are inaccessible.

Common Denial-of-Service Attacks

There are many different methods for carrying out a DoS attack.

The most common method of attack occurs when an attacker floods a network server with traffic.

In this type of DoS attack, the attacker sends several requests to the target server, overloading it with traffic.

These service requests are illegitimate and have fabricated return addresses, which mislead the server when it tries to authenticate the requestor.

As the junk requests are processed constantly, the server is overwhelmed, which causes a DoS condition to legitimate requestors.

In a **Smurf Attack**, the attacker sends Internet Control Message Protocol broadcast packets to a number of hosts with a spoofed source Internet Protocol (IP) address that belongs to the target machine.

The recipients of these spoofed packets will then respond, and the targeted host will be flooded with those responses.

A **SYN flood** occurs when an attacker sends a request to connect to the target server, but never completes the connection through what is known as a three-way handshake—a method used in a TCP/IP network to create a connection between a local host/client and server.

The incomplete handshake leaves the connected port in an occupied status and unavailable for further requests.

An attacker will continue to send requests, saturating all open ports, so that legitimate users cannot connect.

Individual networks may be affected by DoS attacks without being directly targeted.

If the network's internet service provider (ISP) or cloud service provider has been targeted and attacked, the network will also experience a loss of service.

What is a Distributed Denial-of-Service attack?

A distributed denial-of-service or DDoS attack occurs when multiple machines are operating together to attack one target.

DDoS allows for exponentially more requests to be sent to the target, therefore increasing the attack power.

It also increases the difficulty of attribution, as the true source of the attack is harder to identify.

DDoS attackers often leverage the use of a botnet which is a group of hijacked internet-connected devices to carry out large scale attacks.

Attackers take advantage of security vulnerabilities or device weaknesses to control numerous devices using command and control software.

Once in control, an attacker can command their botnet to conduct DDoS on a target. In this case, the infected devices are also victims of the attack.

Once established, the botnet—made up of compromised devices—may also be rented out to other potential attackers.

Often the botnet is made available to "attack-for-hire" services which allow even the most unskilled user to launch DDoS attacks.

DDoS attacks have increased in magnitude as more and more devices come online through the Internet of Things or IoT.

IoT devices often utilize default passwords and do not have sound security postures, making them vulnerable to compromise and exploitation.

Infection of IoT devices often goes unnoticed by users, and an attacker could easily compromise hundreds of thousands of these devices to conduct a high-scale attack without the device owners' knowledge.

How do you avoid being part of the problem?

While there is no way to completely avoid becoming a target of a DoS or DDoS attack, there are proactive steps administrators can take to reduce the effects of an attack on their network.

Enroll in a DoS protection service that will detect abnormal traffic flows and redirect traffic away from your network.

The DoS traffic is then filtered out, while clean traffic is passed on to your network.

Create a disaster recovery plan to ensure successful and efficient communication, mitigation, and recovery in the event of an attack.

It is also important to take steps to strengthen the security posture of all of your internet-connected devices in order to prevent them from being compromised.

Install and maintain antivirus software.

Install a firewall and configure it to restrict traffic coming into and leaving your computer.

Evaluate security settings and follow good security practices in order to minimize the access other people have to your information, as well as manage unwanted traffic.

How do you know if an attack is happening?

Symptoms of a DoS attack can resemble non-malicious availability issues, such as technical problems with a particular network or a system administrator performing maintenance.

However, the following symptoms could indicate a DoS or DDoS attack:

Unusually slow network performance such as when opening files or accessing websites.

Unavailability of a particular website.

An inability to access any website.

The best way to detect and identify a DoS attack would be via network traffic monitoring and analysis.

Network traffic can be monitored via a firewall or intrusion detection system.

An administrator may even set up rules that create an alert upon the detection of an anomalous traffic load and identify the source of the traffic or drops network packets that meet a certain criteria.

What do you do if you think you are experiencing an attack?

If you think you or your business is experiencing a DoS or DDoS attack, it is important to contact the appropriate technical professionals for assistance.

Contact your Network Administrator to confirm whether the service outage is due to maintenance or an in-house network issue.

They can also monitor network traffic to confirm the presence of an attack, identify the source and mitigate the situation by applying firewall rules and possibly rerouting traffic through a DoS protection service.

Contact your ISP to ask if there is an outage on their end or even if their network is the target of the attack and you are an indirect victim.

They may be able to advise you on an appropriate course of action.

In the case of an attack, do not lose sight of the other hosts, assets, or services residing on your network.

Many attackers conduct DoS or DDoS attacks to deflect attention away from their intended target and use the opportunity to conduct secondary attacks on other services within your network

Now you know the basics about denial-of-service attacks.

Risks of File-Sharing Technology

Let's talk about the Risks of File-Sharing Technology

File-sharing technology is a popular way for users to exchange, or "share" files.

However, using this technology makes you susceptible to risks such as infection, attack, or exposure of personal information.

What is file sharing?

File sharing involves using technology that allows internet users to share files that are housed on their individual computers.

Peer-to-peer or P2P applications, such as those used to share music files, are some of the most common forms of file-sharing technology.

However, P2P applications introduce security risks that may put your information or your computer in jeopardy.

What risks does file-sharing technology introduce?

Installation of malicious code

When you use P2P applications, it is difficult, if not impossible, to verify that the source of the files is trustworthy.

These applications are often used by attackers to transmit malicious code.

Attackers may incorporate spyware, viruses, Trojan horses, or worms into the files.

When you download the files, your computer becomes infected.

Exposure of sensitive or personal information

By using P2P applications, you may be giving other users access to personal information.

Whether it's because certain directories are accessible or because you provide personal information to what you believe to be a trusted person or organization, unauthorized people may be able to access your financial or medical data, personal documents, sensitive corporate information, or other personal information.

Once information has been exposed to unauthorized people, it's difficult to know how many people have accessed it.

The availability of this information may increase your risk of identity theft.

Susceptibility to attack

Some P2P applications may ask you to open certain ports on your firewall to transmit the files.

However, opening some of these ports may give attackers access to your computer or enable them to attack your computer by taking advantage of any vulnerabilities that may exist in the P2P application.

There are some P2P applications that can modify and penetrate firewalls themselves, without your knowledge.

Denial of service

Downloading files causes a significant amount of traffic over the network.

This activity may reduce the availability of certain programs on your computer or may limit your access to the internet.

Prosecution

Files shared through P2P applications may include pirated software, copyrighted material, or pornography.

If you download these, even unknowingly, you may be faced with fines or other legal action.

If your computer is on a company network and exposes customer information, both you and your company may be liable.

How can you minimize these risks?

The best way to eliminate these risks is to avoid using P2P applications.

However, if you choose to use this technology, you can follow some good security practices to minimize your risk:

Use and maintain anti-virus software

Anti-virus software recognizes and protects your computer against most known viruses.

However, attackers are continually writing new viruses, so it is important to keep your antivirus software current.

.Install or enable a firewall

Firewalls may be able to prevent some types of infection by blocking malicious traffic before it can enter your computer.

Some operating systems actually include a firewall, but you need to make sure it is enabled.

Now you know the basics about the risks of using file sharing technology.

Avoiding The Pitfalls of Online Trading

Let's talk about Avoiding the Pitfalls of Online Trading.

Online trading can be an easy, cost-effective way to manage investments.

However, online investors are often targets of scams, so take precautions to ensure that you do not become a victim.

What is online trading?

Online trading allows you to conduct investment transactions over the internet.

The accessibility of the internet makes it possible for you to research and invest in opportunities from any location at any time.

It also reduces the amount of resources like time, effort, and money that you have to devote to managing these accounts and transactions.

What are the risks?

Recognizing the importance of safeguarding your money, legitimate brokerages take steps to ensure that their transactions are secure.

However, online brokerages and the investors who use them are appealing targets for attackers.

The amount of financial information in a brokerage's database makes it valuable.

This information can be traded or sold for personal profit.

Also, because money is regularly transferred through these accounts, malicious activity may not be noticed immediately.

To gain access to these databases, attackers may use Trojan horses or other types of malicious code.

Attackers may also attempt to collect financial information by targeting the current or potential investors directly.

These attempts may take the form of social engineering or phishing attacks.

With methods that include setting up fraudulent investment opportunities or redirecting users to malicious sites that appear to be legitimate.

Then attackers try to convince you to provide them with financial information that they can then use or sell.

If you have been victimized, both your money and your identity may be at risk.

How can you protect yourself?

Research your investment opportunities.

Take advantage of resources such as the U.S. Securities and Exchange Commission's EDGAR database and your state's securities commission found through the North American Securities Administrators Association to investigate companies.

Be wary of online information.

Anyone can publish information on the internet, so try to verify any online research through other methods before investing any money.

Also be cautious of "hot" investment opportunities advertised online or in email.

Check privacy policies.

Before providing personal or financial information, check the website's privacy policy.

Make sure you understand how your information will be stored and used.

Read Protecting Your Privacy for more information.

Conduct transactions on devices you control.

Avoid conducting transactions on public resources such as internet kiosks, computers in places like libraries, and other shared computers and devices.

Other users may introduce security risks.

Make sure that your transactions are encrypted.

When information is sent over the internet, attackers may be able to intercept it.

Encryption prevents the attackers from being able to view the information.

Verify that the website is legitimate.

Attackers may redirect you to a malicious website that looks identical to a legitimate one.

They then convince you to submit your personal and financial information, which they use for their own gain.

Check the website's certificate to make sure it is legitimate.

Read Understanding Web Site Certificates for more information.

Monitor your investments.

Regularly check your accounts for any unusual activity.

Report unauthorized transactions immediately.

Use strong passwords.

Protect your computer, mobile devices, and accounts with passwords that cannot easily be guessed.

Use different passwords for each account.

Use and maintain anti-virus software.

Anti-virus software recognizes and protects your computer against most known viruses.

However, because attackers are continually writing new viruses, it is important to keep your virus definitions current.

Use anti-spyware tools.

Spyware is a common source of viruses, and attackers may use it to access information on your computer.

You can minimize the number of infections by using a legitimate program that identifies and removes spyware.

Keep software up to date.

Install software updates so that attackers can't take advantage of known problems or vulnerabilities.

Enable automatic updates if the option is available.

Evaluate your security settings.

By adjusting the security settings in your browser, you may limit your risk of certain attacks.

Now you know the basics about avoiding the pitfalls of online trading.

Avoiding Copyright Infringement

Let's talk about Avoiding Copyright Infringement.

Although copyright may seem to be a purely legal issue, using unauthorized files could have security implications.

To avoid prosecution and minimize the risks to your computer, make sure you have permission to use any copyrighted information, and only download authorized files.

How does copyright infringement apply to the internet?

Copyright infringement occurs when you use or distribute information without permission from the person or organization that owns the legal rights to the information.

Including an image or cartoon on your website or in a document, illegally downloading music, and pirating software are all common copyright violations.

While these activities may seem harmless, they could have serious legal and security implications.

How do you know if you have permission to use something?

If you find something on a website that you would like to use like a document, a chart, or an application, search for information about permissions to use, download, redistribute, or reproduce.

Most websites have a "terms of use" page that explains how you are allowed to use information from the site.

You can often find a link to this page in the site's contact information or privacy policy, or at the bottom of

---

the page that contains the information you are interested in using.

There may be restrictions based on the purpose, method, and audience.

You may also have to adhere to specific conditions about how much information you are allowed to use or how the information is presented and attributed.

If you can't locate the terms of use, or if it seems unclear, contact the individual or organization that holds the copyright to ask permission.

What consequences could you face?

Prosecution.

When you illegally download, reproduce, or distribute information, you risk legal action.

Penalties may range from warnings and mandatory removal of all references to costly fines.

Depending on the severity of the crime, jail time may also be a possibility.

To offset their own court costs and the money they feel they lose because of pirated software, vendors may increase the prices of their products.

Infection.

Attackers could take advantage of sites or networks that offer unauthorized downloads like music, movies, or software by including code into the files that would infect your computer once it was installed.

Because you wouldn't know the source or identity of the infection or maybe that it was even there, you might not be able to easily identify or remove it.

Pirated software with hidden Trojan horses is often advertised as discounted software in spam email messages.

Read "Why is Cyber Security a Problem?" and "Reducing Spam" for more information.

Now you know the basics of avoiding copyright infringement.

Reviewing End-User License Agreements

Let's talk about the importance of reviewing End-User License Agreements

Before accepting an end-user license agreement, make sure you understand and are comfortable with the terms of the agreement.

What is an end-user license agreement?

An end-user license agreement (EULA) is a contract between you and the software's vendor or developer.

Some software packages state that by simply removing the shrink-wrap on the package, you agree to the contract.

However, you may be more familiar with the type of EULA that is presented as a dialog box that appears the first time you open the software.

It usually requires you to accept the conditions of the contract before you can proceed.

Software updates and patches may also include new or updated EULAs that have different terms than the original.

Some EULAs only apply to certain features of the software, so you may only encounter them when you attempt to use those features.

Unfortunately, many users don't read EULAs before accepting them.

The terms of each contract differ, and you may be agreeing to conditions that you later consider unfair or that expose you to security risks you didn't expect.

What terms may be included?

EULAs are legal contracts, and the vendor or developer may include almost any conditions.

These conditions are often designed to protect the developer or vendor against liability, but they may also include additional terms that give the vendor some control over your computer.

The following topics are often covered in EULAs:

Distribution

There are often limitations placed on the number of times you are allowed to install the software and restrictions about reproducing the software for distribution.

Warranty

Developers or vendors often include disclaimers that they are not liable for any problem that results from the software being used incorrectly.

They may also protect themselves from liability for software flaws, software failure, or incompatibility with other programs on your computer.

The following topics, while not standard, are examples of other conditions that have been included in EULAs.

They present security implications that you should consider before accepting the agreement.

Monitoring

Agreeing to the EULA may give the vendor permission to monitor your computer activity and communicate the information back to the vendor or to another third party.

Depending on what information is being collected, this type of monitoring could have both security and privacy implications.

Software installation

Some agreements allow the vendor to install additional software on your computer.

This may include updated versions of the software program you installed.

The determination of which version you are running may be a result of the monitoring described above.

Vendors may also incorporate statements that allow them or other third parties to install additional software programs on your computer.

This software may be unnecessary, may affect the functionality of other programs on your computer, and may introduce security risks.

Now you know the basics about reviewing end-user license agreements.

INSPIRED? READY TO TAKE ACTION AND IMPLEMENT?

It's time to build your security culture anytime, anywhere, on any device. Not only do you get the tools and systems to become one of the most well-defended managed service providers around, you learn the mindset it takes to become successful in cybersecurity and can pass both on to your clients.

You'll also learn more about how you can assess, educate, and monitor your staff. There are hundreds of ways to improve your security based on your unique business. Now is the time to become competition and recession-proof.

Visit www.HailBytes.com for free security resources!

Malicious Emails & Phishing

Understanding Your Computer: Email Clients

The main difference between email clients is the user interface. Regardless of which software you decide to use, follow good security practices when reading or sending email.

How do email clients work?

Every email address has two basic parts: the user name and the domain name. When you are sending email to someone else, your domain's server has to communicate with your recipient's domain server.

For example, let's assume that your email address is *johndoe@example.com*, and the person you are contacting is at *janesmith@anotherexample.org*. In very basic terms, after you hit **send**, the server hosting your domain (example.com) looks at the email address and then contacts the server hosting the recipient's domain (anotherexample.org) to let it know that it has a message for someone at that domain. Once the connection has been established, the server hosting the recipient's domain (anotherexample.org) then looks at the user name of the email address and routes the message to that account.

How many email clients are there?

There are many different email clients and services, each with its own interface. Some are web-based applications, some are stand-alone applications installed directly on your computer, and some are text-based applications. There are also variations of many of these email clients that have been designed specifically for mobile devices such as cell phones.

How do you choose an email client?

There is usually an email client included with the installation of your operating system, but many other alternatives are available. Be wary of "home-brewed" software, because it may not be as secure or reliable as software that is tested and actively maintained. Some of the factors to consider when deciding which email client best suits your needs include

Security

Do you feel that your email program offers you the level of security you want for sending, receiving, and reading email messages? How does it handle attachments? If you are dealing with sensitive information, do you have the option of sending and receiving signed and/or encrypted messages?

Privacy

If you are using a web-based service, have you read its privacy policy? Do you know what information is being collected and who has access to it? Are there options for filtering spam?

Functionality

Does the software send, receive, and interpret email messages appropriately?

Reliability

For web-based services, is the server reliable, or is your email frequently unavailable due to maintenance, security problems, a high volume of users, or other reasons?

Availability

Do you need to be able to access your account from any computer?

Ease of use

Are the menus and options easy to understand and use?

Visual appeal

Do you find the interface appealing?

Each email client may have a different way of organizing drafted, sent, saved, and deleted mail. Familiarize yourself with the software so that you can find and store messages easily, and so that you don't unintentionally lose messages. Once you have chosen the software you want to use for your email, protect yourself and your contacts by following good security practices.

Can you use more than one email client?

You can have more than one email client, although you may have issues with compatibility. Some email accounts, such as those issued through your internet service provider (ISP) or place of employment, are only accessible from a computer that has appropriate privileges and settings for you to access that account. You can use any stand-alone email client to read those messages, but if you have more than one client installed on your machine, you should choose one as your default. When you click an email link in a browser or email message, your computer will open that default email client that you chose.

Most vendors give you the option to download their email software directly from their websites. Make sure to verify the authenticity of the site before downloading any files, and follow other good security practices, like using a firewall and keeping anti-virus software up to date, to further minimize risk.

You can also maintain free email accounts through browser-based email clients (e.g., Yahoo!, Hotmail, Gmail) that you can access from any computer. Because these accounts are maintained directly on the vendors' servers, they don't interfere with other email accounts.

Using Caution with Email Attachments

Let's talk about using Caution with Email Attachments.

While email attachments are a popular and convenient way to send documents, they are also one of the most common sources of viruses.

Use caution when opening attachments, even if they appear to have been sent by someone you know.

Why can email attachments be dangerous?

Some of the characteristics that make email attachments convenient and popular are also the ones that make them a common tool for attackers:

Email is easily circulated.

Forwarding email is so simple that viruses can quickly infect many machines.

Most viruses don't even require users to forward the email.

Instead they scan a users' computer for email addresses and automatically send the infected message to all of the addresses they find.

Attackers take advantage of the reality that most users will automatically trust and open any message that comes from someone they know.

Email programs try to address all users' needs.

Almost any type of file can be attached to an email message, so attackers have more freedom with the types of viruses they can send.

Email programs offer many "user-friendly" features.

Some email programs have the option to automatically download email attachments, which immediately exposes your computer to any viruses within the attachments.

What steps can you take to protect yourself and others in your address book?

Be wary of unsolicited attachments, even from people you know.

Just because an email message looks like it came from your mom, grandma, or boss doesn't mean that it did.

Many viruses can "spoof" the return address, making it look like the message came from someone else.

If you can, check with the person who supposedly sent the message to make sure it's legitimate before opening any attachments.

This includes email messages that appear to be from your ISP or software vendor and claim to include patches or anti-virus software.

ISPs and software vendors do not send patches or software in email.

Keep software up to date.

Install software patches so that attackers can't take advantage of known problems or vulnerabilities.

Many operating systems offer automatic updates.

If this option is available, you should enable it.

Trust your instincts.

If an email or email attachment seems suspicious, don't open it.

Even if your anti-virus software indicates that the message is clean.

Attackers are constantly releasing new viruses, and the anti-virus software might not have the right "signature" to recognize a new virus.

At the very least, contact the person who supposedly sent the message to make sure it's legitimate before you open the attachment.

However, especially in the case of forwards, even messages sent by a legitimate sender might contain a virus.

If something about the email or the attachment makes you uncomfortable, there may be a good reason.

Don't let your curiosity put your computer at risk.

Save and scan any attachments before opening them.

If you have to open an attachment before you can verify the source, take the following steps:

Be sure the signatures in your anti-virus software are up to date.

Save the file to your computer or a disk.

Manually scan the file using your anti-virus software.

If the file is clean and doesn't seem suspicious, go ahead and open it.

Turn off the option to automatically download attachments.

To simplify the process of reading email, many email programs offer the feature to automatically download attachments.

Check your settings to see if your software offers the option, and make sure to disable it.

Consider creating separate accounts on your computer.

Most operating systems give you the option of creating multiple user accounts with different privileges.

Consider reading your email on an account with restricted privileges.

Some viruses need "administrator" privileges to infect a computer.

Apply additional security practices.

You may be able to filter certain types of attachments through your email software or a firewall.

Now you know how to use caution when dealing with email attachments.

Reducing Spam

Let's take a minute to talk about Reducing Spam.

Spam is a common, and often frustrating, side effect to having an email account.

Although you will probably not be able to eliminate it, there are ways to reduce it.

What is spam?

Spam is the electronic version of "junk mail."

The term spam refers to unsolicited, often unwanted, email messages.

Spam does not necessarily contain viruses.

Valid messages from legitimate sources could fall into this category.

How can you reduce the amount of spam?

Be careful about releasing your email address.

Think twice before you respond to any request for your email address, on the web, verbally, or on paper.

Spammers can harvest any email address posted on a website.

If you give your email address to a company, that information is often entered into a database so that customer information and preferences can be tracked.

If these email databases are sold to or shared with other companies, you can receive email that you didn't request.

Check privacy policies.

Before submitting your email address online, look for a privacy policy.

Most reputable sites will have a link to their privacy policy from any form where you're asked to submit personal data.

You should read this policy before submitting your email address or any other personal information so that you know what the owners of the site plan to do with the information.

Be aware of options selected by default.

When you sign up for some online accounts or services, there may be a section that provides you with the option to receive email about other products and services.

Sometimes there are options selected by default, so if you do not deselect them, you could begin to receive email from those lists as well.

Use filters or spam tagging.

Many email programs offer filtering capabilities that allow you to block certain addresses or to allow only email from addresses on your contact list.

Many ISPs also offer spam tagging services that allow the user the option to review suspected spam messages before they are deleted.

Spam tagging can be useful in conjunction with filtering capabilities provided by many email programs.

Report messages as spam.

Most email clients offer an option to report a message as spam or junk.

If your email client has that option, take advantage of it.

Reporting messages as spam or junk helps to train the mail filter so that the messages aren't delivered to your inbox.

However, check your junk or spam folders occasionally to look for legitimate messages that were incorrectly classified as spam.

Don't follow links in spam messages.

Some spam relies on generators that try variations of email addresses at certain domains.

If you click a link within an email message or reply to a certain address, you are just confirming that your email address is valid.

Unwanted messages that offer an "unsubscribe" option are particularly tempting, but this is often just a method for collecting valid addresses that are then targeted for other spam.

Disable the automatic downloading of graphics in HTML mail.

Many spammers send HTML mail with a linked graphic file that is then used to track who opens the mail message.

When your mail client downloads the graphic from their web server, the spammers know you've opened the message.

Disabling HTML mail entirely and viewing messages in plain text also prevents this problem.

Consider opening an additional email account.

Many domains offer free email accounts.

If you frequently submit your email address (for online shopping, signing up for services, or including it on something like a comment card), you may want to have a secondary email account to protect your primary email account from any spam that could be generated.

You could also use this secondary account when posting to public mailing lists, social networking sites, blogs, and web forums.

If the account starts to fill up with spam, you can get rid of it and open a different one.

Use privacy settings on social networking sites

Social networking sites typically allow you to choose who has access to see your email address.

Consider hiding your email account or changing the settings so that only a small group of people that you trust are able to see your address. (See Staying Safe on Social Networking Sites for more information.)

Know that when you use applications on these sites, you may be granting permission for them to access your personal information.

So, be cautious about which applications you choose to use.

Don't spam other people

Be a responsible and considerate user.

Some people consider email forwards a type of spam, so be selective with the messages you redistribute.

Don't forward every message to everyone in your address book, and if recipients ask that you not forward messages to them, respect their requests.

Benefits of BCC

Let's talk about the Benefits of BCC for your emails.

Although in many situations it may be appropriate to list email recipients in the To: or CC: fields, sometimes using the BCC: field may be the most desirable option.

What is BCC?

BCC, which stands for blind carbon copy, allows you to hide recipients in email messages.

Addresses in the To: field and the CC: (carbon copy) field appear in messages, but users cannot see addresses of anyone you included in the BCC: field.

Why would you want to use BCC?

There are a few main reasons for using BCC:

Privacy.

Sometimes it's beneficial, even necessary, for you to let recipients know who else is receiving your email message.

However, there may be instances when you want to send the same message to multiple recipients without letting them know who else is receiving the message.

If you are sending email on behalf of a business or organization, it may be especially important to keep lists of clients, members, or associates confidential.

You may also want to avoid listing an internal email address on a message being sent to external recipients.

Another point to remember is that if any of the recipients use the "reply to all" feature to reply to your messages, all of the recipients listed in the To: and CC: fields will receive the reply.

If there is potential for a response that is not appropriate for all recipients, consider using BCC.

Tracking.

Maybe you want to access or archive the email message you are sending at another email account.

Or maybe you want to make someone, such as a supervisor or team member, aware of the email without actually involving them in the exchange.   .

BCC allows you to accomplish these goals without advertising that you are doing it.

Respect for your recipients.

People often forward email messages without removing the addresses of previous recipients.

As a result, messages that are repeatedly sent to many recipients may contain long lists of email addresses.

Spammers and email-borne viruses may collect and target those addresses.

To reduce the risk, encourage people who forward messages to you to use BCC so that your email address is less likely to appear in other people's inboxes and be susceptible to being harvested.

To avoid becoming part of the problem, in addition to using BCC if you forward messages, take time to remove all existing email addresses within the message.

The additional benefit is that the people you're sending the message to will appreciate not having to scroll through large sections of irrelevant information to get to the actual message.

How do you BCC an email message?

Most email clients have the option to BCC listed a few lines below the To: field.

However, sometimes it is a separate option that is not listed by default.

If you cannot locate it, check the help menu or the software's documentation.

If you want to BCC all recipients and your email client will not send a message without something in the To: field, consider using your own email address in that field.

In addition to hiding the identity of other recipients, this option will enable you to confirm that the message was sent successfully.

Now you understand the benefits of BCC.

Benefits and Risks of Free Email Services

Although free email services are convenient for sending personal correspondence, you should not use them to send messages containing sensitive information.

What is the appeal of free email services?

Many service providers offer free email accounts like Yahoo!, Hotmail, and Gmail.

These email services typically provide you with a browser interface to access your mail.

In addition to the monetary savings, these services often offer other benefits:

Accessibility.

Because you can access your accounts from any computer, these services are useful if you cannot be near your computer or are in the process of relocating and do not have an ISP.

Even if you are able to access your ISP-based email account remotely, being able to rely on a free email account is ideal if you are using a public computer or a shared wireless hotspot and are concerned about exposing the details of your primary account.

Competitive features.

With so many of these service providers competing for users, they now offer additional features such as large amounts of storage, spam filtering, virus protection, and enhanced fonts and graphics.

Additional capabilities.

It is becoming more common for service providers to package additional software or services like instant messaging with their free email accounts to attract customers.

Free email accounts are also effective tools for reducing the amount of spam you receive at your primary email address.

Instead of submitting your primary address when shopping online, requesting services, or participating in online forums, you can set up a free secondary address to use.

Read Reducing Spam for more information.

What risks are associated with free email services?

Although free email services have many benefits, you should not use them to send sensitive information.

Because you are not paying for the account, the organization may not have a strong commitment to protecting you from various threats or to offering you the best service.

Some of the elements you risk are:

Security.

If your login, password, or messages are sent in plain text, they may easily be intercepted.

If a service provider offers SSL encryption, you should use it.

You can find out whether this is available by looking for a "secure mode" or by replacing the "http:" in the URL with "https:".

Read Protecting Your Privacy for more information.

Privacy.

You aren't paying for your email account, but the service provider has to find some way to recover the costs of providing the service.

One way of generating revenue is to sell advertising space, but another is to sell or trade information.

Make sure to read the service provider's privacy policy or terms of use to see if your name, your email address, the email addresses in your address book, or any of the information in your profile has the potential of being given to other organizations.

Read Protecting Your Privacy for more information.

If you are considering forwarding your work email to a free email account, check with your employer first.

You do not want to violate any established security policies.

Reliability.

Although you may be able to access your account from any computer, you need to make sure that the account is going to be available when you want to access it.

Familiarize yourself with the service provider's terms of service so that you know exactly what they have committed to providing you.

For example, if the service ends or your account disappears, can you retrieve your messages?

Does the service provider give you the ability to download messages that you want to archive onto your machine?

Also, if you happen to be in a different time zone than the provider, you may find that their server maintenance interferes with your normal email routine.

INSPIRED? READY TO TAKE ACTION AND IMPLEMENT?

It's time to build your security culture anytime, anywhere, on any device. Not only do you get the tools and systems to become one of the most well-defended managed service providers around, you learn the

---

mindset it takes to become successful in cybersecurity and can pass both on to your clients.

You'll also learn more about how you can assess, educate, and monitor your staff. There are hundreds of ways to improve your security based on your unique business. Now is the time to become competition and recession-proof.

Visit www.HailBytes.com for free security resources!

Malicious Software

Ensure Endpoint Security.

Just as a chain is only as strong as its weakest link, your network security is only as strong as the weakest security on a computer with remote access to it. That's the message of FTC cases in which companies failed to ensure that computers with remote access to their networks had appropriate endpoint security. For example, in Premier Capital Lending, the company allegedly activated a remote login account for a business client to obtain consumer reports, without first assessing the business's security. When hackers accessed the client's system, they stole its remote login credentials and used them to grab consumers' personal information. According to the complaint in Settlement One, the business allowed clients that didn't have basic security measures, like firewalls and updated antivirus software, to access consumer reports through its online portal. And in Lifelock, the FTC charged that the company failed to install antivirus programs on the computers that employees used to remotely access its network. These businesses could have reduced those risks by securing computers that had remote access to their networks.

Understanding Patches and Software Updates

When vendors become aware of vulnerabilities in their products, they often issue patches to fix those vulnerabilities. Make sure to apply relevant patches to your computer as soon as possible so that your system is protected.

What are patches?

Patches are software and operating system (OS) updates that address security vulnerabilities within a program or product. Software vendors may choose to release updates to fix performance bugs, as well as to provide enhanced security features.

How do you find out what software updates you need to install?

When software updates become available, vendors usually put them on their websites for users to download. Install updates as soon as possible to protect your computer, phone, or other digital device against attackers who would take advantage of system vulnerabilities. Attackers may target vulnerabilities for months or even years after updates are available.

Some software will automatically check for updates, and many vendors offer users the option to receive updates automatically. If automatic options are available, NCCIC recommends that you take advantage of them. If they are not available, periodically check your vendor's websites for updates.

Make sure that you only download software updates from trusted vendor websites. Do not trust a link in an email message—attackers have used email messages to direct users to websites hosting malicious files disguised as legitimate updates. Users should also be suspicious of email messages that claim to have a software update file attached—these attachments may contain malware (see Using Caution with Email Attachments for more information).

If possible, only apply automatic updates from trusted network locations (e.g., home, work). Avoid updating software (automatically or manually) while connected to untrusted networks (e.g., airport, hotel, coffee shop). If updates must be installed over an untrusted network, use a Virtual Private Network connection to a trusted network and apply updates.

What is the difference between manual and automatic updates?

Users can install updates manually or elect for their software programs to update automatically.

- Manual updates require the user or administrator to visit the vendor's website to download and install software files.
- Automatic updates require user or administrator consent when installing or configuring the software. Once you consent to automatic updates, software updates are "pushed" (or installed) to your system automatically.

What is end-of-life software?

Sometimes vendors will discontinue support for a software program or issue software updates for it (also known as end-of-life [EOL] software). Continued use of EOL software poses consequential risk to your system that can allow an attacker to exploit security vulnerabilities present that could result in malware attacks. The use of unsupported software can also cause software compatibility issues as well as decreased system performance and productivity.

NCCIC recommends that users and administrators retire all EOL products.

Best Practices for Software Updates

•   Enable automatic software updates whenever possible. This will ensure that software updates are installed as quickly as possible.
•   Do not use unsupported EOL software.
•   Always visit vendor sites directly rather than clicking on advertisements or email links.
•   Avoid software updates while using untrusted networks.

New vulnerabilities are continually emerging, but the best defense against attackers exploiting patched vulnerabilities is simple: keep your software up-to-date. This is the most effective measure you can take to protect your computer, phone, and other digital devices.

Understanding Hidden Threats: Rootkits and Botnets

Attackers are continually finding new ways to access computer systems. The use of hidden methods such as rootkits and botnets has increased, and you may be a victim without even realizing it.

What are rootkits and botnets?

A rootkit is a piece of software that can be installed and hidden on your computer without your knowledge.

It may be included in a larger software package or installed by an attacker who has been able to take advantage of a vulnerability on your computer or has convinced you to download it (see Avoiding Social Engineering and Phishing Attacks for more information).

Rootkits are not necessarily malicious, but they may hide malicious activities. Attackers may be able to access information, monitor your actions, modify programs, or perform other functions on your computer without being detected.

Botnet is a term derived from the idea of bot networks. In its most basic form, a bot is simply an automated computer program, or robot. In the context of botnets, bots refer to computers that are able to be controlled by one, or many, outside sources.

An attacker usually gains control by infecting the computers with a virus or other malicious code that gives the attacker access. Your computer may be part of a botnet even though it appears to be operating normally.

Botnets are often used to conduct a range of activities, from distributing spam and viruses to conducting denial-of-service attacks (see Understanding Denial-of-Service Attacks for more information).

Why are they considered threats?

The main problem with both rootkits and botnets is that they are hidden. Although botnets are not hidden the same way rootkits are, they may be undetected unless you are specifically looking for certain activity.

If a rootkit has been installed, you may not be aware that your computer has been compromised, and traditional anti-virus software may not be able to detect the malicious programs. Attackers are also creating more sophisticated programs that update themselves so that they are even harder to detect.

Attackers can use rootkits and botnets to access and modify personal information, attack other computers, and commit other crimes, all while remaining undetected. By using multiple computers, attackers increase the range and impact of their crimes.

Because each computer in a botnet can be programmed to execute the same command, an attacker can have each of them scanning multiple computers for vulnerabilities, monitoring online activity, or collecting the information entered in online forms.

What can you do to protect yourself?

If you practice good security habits, you may reduce the risk that your computer will be compromised:

Use and maintain anti-virus software

Anti-virus software recognizes and protects your computer against most known viruses, so you may be able to detect and remove the virus before it can do any damage (see Understanding Anti-Virus Software for more information). Because attackers are continually writing new viruses, it is important to keep your definitions up to date. Some anti-virus vendors also offer anti-rootkit software.

Install a firewall

Firewalls may be able to prevent some types of infection by blocking malicious traffic before it can enter your computer and limiting the traffic you send (see Understanding Firewalls for more information). Some operating systems actually include a firewall, but you need to make sure it is enabled.

Use good passwords

Select passwords that will be difficult for attackers to guess, and use different passwords for different programs and devices (see Choosing and Protecting Passwords for more information). Do not choose options that allow your computer to remember your passwords.

Keep software up to date

Install software patches so that attackers can't take advantage of known problems or vulnerabilities (see Understanding Patches for more information). Many operating systems offer automatic updates. If this option is available, you should enable it.

Follow good security practices

Take appropriate precautions when using email and web browsers to reduce the risk that your actions will trigger an infection.

Unfortunately, if there is a rootkit on your computer or an attacker is using your computer in a botnet, you may not know it.

Even if you do discover that you are a victim, it is difficult for the average user to effectively recover.

The attacker may have modified files on your computer, so simply removing the malicious files may not solve the problem, and you may not be able to safely trust a prior version of a file.

If you believe that you are a victim, consider contacting a trained system administrator.

As an alternative, some vendors are developing products and tools that may remove a rootkit from your computer.

If the software cannot locate and remove the infection, you may need to reinstall your operating system, usually with a system restore disk that is often supplied with a new computer.

Note that reinstalling or restoring the operating system typically erases all of your files and any additional software that you have installed on your computer.

Also, the infection may be located at such a deep level that it cannot be removed by simply reinstalling or restoring the operating system.

Understanding Hidden Threats: Corrupted Software Files

Malicious code is not always hidden in web page scripts or unusual file formats. Attackers may corrupt types of files that you would recognize and typically consider safe, so you should take precautions when opening files from other people.

What types of files can attackers corrupt?

An attacker may be able to insert malicious code into any file, including common file types that you would normally consider safe.

These files may include documents created with word processing software, spreadsheets, or image files. After corrupting the file, an attacker may distribute it through email or post it to a website. Depending on the type of malicious code, you may infect your computer by just opening the file.

When corrupting files, attackers often take advantage of vulnerabilities that they discover in the software that is used to create or open the file.

These vulnerabilities may allow attackers to insert and execute malicious scripts or code, and they are not always detected. Sometimes the vulnerability involves a combination of certain files (such as a particular piece of software running on a particular operating system) or only affects certain versions of a software program.

What problems can malicious files cause?

There are various types of malicious code, including viruses, worms, and Trojan horses (see What is Cybersecurity? for more information). However, the range of consequences varies even within these categories. The malicious code may be designed to perform one or more functions, including

- interfering with your computer's ability to process information by consuming memory or bandwidth (causing your computer to become significantly slower or even "freeze")
- installing, altering, or deleting files on your computer
- giving the attacker access to your computer
- using your computer to attack other computers (see Understanding Denial-of-Service Attacks for more information)

How can you protect yourself?

Use and maintain anti-virus software

Anti-virus software can often recognize and protect your computer against most known viruses, so you may be able to detect and remove the virus before it can do any damage (see Understanding Anti-Virus Software for more information). Because attackers are continually writing new viruses, it is important to keep your definitions up to date.

Use caution with email attachments

Do not open email attachments that you were not expecting, especially if they are from people you do not know. If you decide to open an email attachment, scan it for viruses first (see Using Caution with Email Attachments for more information). Not only is it possible for attackers to "spoof" the source of an email message, but your legitimate contacts may unknowingly send you an infected file. If your email program automatically downloads and opens attachments, check your settings to see if you can disable this feature.

Be wary of downloadable files on websites

Avoid downloading files from sites that you do not trust. If you are getting the files from a supposedly secure site, look for a website certificate (see Understanding Web Site Certificates for more information). If you do download a file from a website, consider saving it to your computer and manually scanning it for viruses before opening it.

Keep software up to date

Install software patches so that attackers cannot take advantage of known problems or vulnerabilities (see Understanding Patches for more information). Many operating systems offer automatic updates. If this option is available, you should enable it.

Take advantage of security settings

Check the security settings of your email client and your web browser (see Evaluating Your Web Browser's Security Settings for more information). Apply the highest level of security available that still gives you the functionality you need.

Understanding Anti-Virus Software

Let's take a minute to discuss Understanding Anti-Virus Software.

Anti-virus software can identify and block many viruses before they can infect your computer.

Once you install anti-virus software, it's important to keep it up to date.

What does anti-virus software do?

Although details may vary between packages, antivirus software scans files or your computer's memory for certain patterns that may indicate the presence of malicious software, also known as malware.

Anti-virus software, sometimes more broadly referred to as anti-malware software, looks for patterns based on the signatures or definitions of known malware.

Anti-virus vendors find new and updated malware daily, so it is important that you have the latest updates installed on your computer.

Once you have installed an antivirus package, you should scan your entire computer periodically.

Automatic scans.

Most anti-virus software can be configured to automatically scan specific files or directories in real time and prompt you at set intervals to perform complete scans.

Manual scans.

If your anti-virus software does not automatically scan new files, you should manually scan files and media you receive from an outside source before opening them.

This process includes:

Saving and scanning email attachments or web downloads rather than opening them directly from the source.

Scanning media, including CDs and DVDs, for malware before opening files.

How will the software respond when it finds malware?

Sometimes the software will produce a dialog box alerting you that it has found malware and ask whether you want it to "clean" the file in order to remove the malware.

In other cases, the software may attempt to remove the malware without asking you first.

When you select an antivirus package, familiarize yourself with its features so you know what to expect.

Which software should you use?

There are many vendors who produce anti-virus software, and deciding which one to choose can be confusing.

Anti-virus software typically performs the same types of functions, so your decision may be driven by recommendations, particular features, availability, or price.

Regardless of which package you choose, installing any anti-virus software will increase your level of protection.

How do you get the current malware information?

This process may differ depending on what product you choose, so find out what your anti-virus software requires.

Many anti-virus packages include an option to automatically receive updated malware definitions.

Because new information is added frequently, it is a good idea to take advantage of this option.

Resist believing alarmist emails claiming that the "worst virus in history" or the "most dangerous malware ever" has been detected and will destroy your computer's hard drive.

These emails are usually hoaxes.

You can confirm malware information through your anti-virus vendor or through resources offered by other antivirus vendors.

While installing anti-virus software is one of the easiest and most effective ways to protect your computer, it has its limitations.

Because it relies on signatures, anti-virus software can only detect malware that has known characteristics.

It is important to keep these signatures up-to-date.

You will still be susceptible to malware that circulates before the anti-virus vendors add their signatures, so continue to take other safety precautions as well.

Now you understand the basics of antivirus software.

Recovering from Viruses, Worms, and Trojans

Unfortunately, many users are victims of viruses, worms, or Trojan horses. If your computer gets infected with malicious code, there are steps you can take to recover.

How do you know your computer is infected?

Unfortunately, there is no particular way to identify that your computer has been infected with malicious code. Some infections may completely destroy files and shut down your computer, while others may only subtly affect your computer's normal operations. Be aware of any unusual or unexpected behaviors.

If you are running anti-virus software, it may alert you that it has found malicious code on your computer. The anti-virus software may be able to clean the malicious code automatically, but if it can't, you will need to take additional steps.

What can you do if you are infected?

Minimize the damage

If you are at work and have access to an IT department, contact them immediately. The sooner they can investigate and clean your computer, the less damage to your computer and other computers on the network. If you are on your home computer or a laptop, disconnect your computer from the internet.

By removing the internet connection, you prevent an attacker or virus from being able to access your computer and perform tasks such as locating personal data, manipulating or deleting files, or using your computer to attack other computers.

Remove the malicious code

If you have anti-virus software installed on your computer, update the virus definitions (if possible), and perform a manual scan of your entire system. If you do not have anti-virus software, you can purchase it at a local computer store (see Understanding Anti-Virus Software for more information).

If the software can't locate and remove the infection, you may need to reinstall your operating system, usually with a system restore disk that is often supplied with a new computer.

Note that reinstalling or restoring the operating system typically erases all of your files and any additional software that you have installed on your computer.

After reinstalling the operating system and any other software, install all of the appropriate patches to fix known vulnerabilities (see Understanding Patches for more information).

How can you reduce the risk of another infection?

Dealing with the presence of malicious code on your computer can be a frustrating experience that can cost you time, money, and data. The following recommendations will build your defense against future infections:

Use and maintain anti-virus software

Anti-virus software recognizes and protects your computer against most known viruses. However, attackers are continually writing new viruses, so it is important to keep your antivirus software current (see Understanding Anti-Virus Software for more information).

Change your passwords

Your original passwords may have been compromised during the infection, so you should change them. This includes passwords for web sites that may have been cached in your browser. Make the passwords difficult for attackers to guess (see Choosing and Protecting Passwords for more information).

Keep software up to date

Install software patches so that attackers can't take advantage of known problems or vulnerabilities (see

Understanding Patches for more information). Many operating systems offer automatic updates. If this option is available, you should enable it.

Install or enable a firewall

Firewalls may be able to prevent some types of infection by blocking malicious traffic before it can enter your computer (see Understanding Firewalls for more information). Some operating systems actually include a firewall, but you need to make sure it is enabled.

Use anti-spyware tools

Spyware is a common source of viruses, but you can minimize the number of infections by using a legitimate program that identifies and removes spyware (see Recognizing and Avoiding Spyware for more information).

Follow good security practices

Take appropriate precautions when using email and web browsers so that you reduce the risk that your actions will trigger an infection.

As a precaution, maintain backups of your files on CDs or DVDs so that you have saved copies if you do get infected again

Recognizing Fake Antiviruses

It's important to protect your computer from fake antivirus infections and to be able to recognize when an infection has occurred.

What is fake antivirus?

Fake antivirus is malicious software or malware designed to steal information from unsuspecting users by mimicking legitimate security software.

The malware makes numerous system modifications making it extremely difficult to terminate unauthorized activities and remove the program.

It also causes realistic, interactive security warnings to be displayed to the computer user.

How can my computer become infected with fake antivirus?

Criminals distribute this type of malware using search engines, emails, social networking sites, internet advertisements and other malware.

They leverage advanced social engineering methodologies and popular technologies to maximize the number of infected computers.

How will I know if I am infected?

The presence of pop-ups displaying unusual security warnings and asking for credit card or personal information is the most obvious method of identifying a fake antivirus infection.

What can I do to protect myself?

1. Be cautious when visiting web links or opening attachments from unknown senders.
2. Keep software patched and updated.

3.   To purchase or renew software subscriptions, visit the vendor sites directly.

4.   Monitor your credit cards for unauthorized activity.

5.   To report Internet crime or fraud, contact the Internet Crime Complaint Center at ic3.gov.

Now you know the basics of recognizing and avoiding fake antivirus.

Recognizing and Avoiding Spyware

Because of its popularity, the internet has become an ideal target for advertising.

As a result, spyware, or adware, has become increasingly prevalent.

When troubleshooting problems with your computer, you may discover that the source of the problem is spyware software that has been installed on your machine without your knowledge.

What is spyware?

Despite its name, the term "spyware" doesn't refer to something used by undercover operatives, but rather by the advertising industry.

In fact, spyware is also known as "adware."

It refers to a category of software that, when installed on your computer, may send you pop-up ads, redirect your browser to certain websites, or monitor the web sites that you visit.

Some extreme, invasive versions of spyware may track exactly what keys you type.

This type of software is also known as a keylogger.

Attackers may also use spyware for malicious purposes.

Because of the extra processing, spyware may cause your computer to become slow or sluggish.

There are also privacy implications:

What information is being gathered?

Who is receiving it?

How is it being used?

How do you know if there is spyware on your computer?

The following symptoms may indicate that spyware is installed on your computer:

1.   you are subjected to endless pop-up windows
2.   you are redirected to websites other than the one you typed into your browser
3.   new, unexpected toolbars appear in your web browser
4.   new, unexpected icons appear in the task tray at the bottom of your screen
5.   your browser's homepage suddenly changed
6.   the search engine your browser opens when you click "search" has been changed
7.   certain keys fail to work in your browser, for example the tab key doesn't work when you are moving to the next field within a form.
8.   random Windows error messages begin to appear
9.   your computer suddenly seems very slow when opening programs or processing tasks like saving files.

How can you prevent spyware from installing on your computer?

To avoid unintentionally installing it yourself, follow these good security practices:

Don't click on links within pop-up windows

Because pop-up windows are often a product of spyware, clicking on the window may install spyware software on your computer. To close the pop-up window, click on the "X" icon in the title bar instead of a "close" link within the window.

Choose "no" when asked unexpected questions

Be wary of unexpected dialog boxes asking whether you want to run a particular program or perform another type of task. Always select "no" or "cancel," or close the dialog box by clicking the "X" icon in the title bar.

Be wary of free downloadable software

There are many sites that offer customized toolbars or other features that appeal to users. Don't download programs from sites you don't trust, and realize that you may be exposing your computer to spyware by downloading some of these programs.

Don't follow email links claiming to offer anti-spyware software

Like email viruses, the links may serve the opposite purpose and actually install the spyware it claims to be eliminating.

As an additional good security practice, especially if you are concerned that you might have spyware on your machine and want to minimize the impact, consider **Adjusting your browser preferences to limit pop-up windows and cookies**.

Pop-up windows are often generated by some kind of scripting or active content.

Adjusting the settings within your browser to reduce or prevent scripting or active content may reduce the number of pop-up windows that appear.

Some browsers offer a specific option to block or limit pop-up windows.

Certain types of cookies are sometimes considered spyware because they reveal what web pages you have visited.

You can adjust your privacy settings to only allow cookies for the web site you are visiting.

How do you remove spyware?

Run a full scan on your computer with your antivirus software

Some anti-virus software will find and remove spyware, but it may not find the spyware when it is monitoring your computer in real time.

Set your anti-virus software to prompt you to run a full scan periodically.

Run a legitimate product specifically designed to remove spyware

Many vendors offer products that will scan your computer for spyware and remove any spyware software.

Popular products include Lavasoft's Ad-Aware, Microsoft's Window Defender, Webroot's SpySweeper, and Spybot Search and Destroy.

Make sure that your anti-virus and anti-spyware software are compatible

Take a phased approach to installing the software to ensure that you don't unintentionally introduce problems.

Now you understand the basics of recognizing and avoiding spyware.

Protecting Against Malicious Code

Protect yourself from unwanted, and potentially harmful, files or programs by following cybersecurity best practices.

What is malicious code?

Malicious code is unwanted files or programs that can cause harm to a computer or compromise data stored

---

Visit www.HailBytes.com for free cybersecurity resources!

on a computer. Various classifications of malicious code include viruses, worms, and Trojan horses.

- **Viruses** have the ability to damage or destroy files on a computer system and are spread by sharing an already infected removable media, opening malicious email attachments, and visiting malicious web pages.
- **Worms** are a type of virus that self-propagates from computer to computer. Its functionality is to use all of your computer's resources, which can cause your computer to stop responding.
- **Trojan Horses** are computer programs that are hiding a virus or a potentially damaging program. It is not uncommon that free software contains a Trojan horse making a user think they are using legitimate software, instead the program is performing malicious actions on your computer.
- **Malicious data files** are non-executable files—such as a Microsoft Word document, an Adobe PDF, a ZIP file, or an image file—that exploits weaknesses in the software program used to open it. Attackers frequently use malicious data files to install malware on a victim's system, commonly distributing the files via email, social media, and websites.

How can you protect yourself against malicious code?

Following these security practices can help you reduce the risks associated with malicious code:

Install and maintain antivirus software.

Antivirus software recognizes malware and protects your computer against it. Installing antivirus software from a reputable vendor is an important step in preventing and detecting infections.

Always visit vendor sites directly rather than clicking on advertisements or email links. Because attackers are continually creating new viruses and other forms of malicious code, it is important to keep your antivirus software up-to-date.

Use caution with links and attachments.

Take appropriate precautions when using email and web browsers to reduce the risk of an infection. Be wary of unsolicited email attachments and use caution when clicking on email links, even if they seem to come from people you know. (See Using Caution with Email Attachments for more information.)

Block pop-up advertisements.

Pop-up blockers disable windows that could potentially contain malicious code. Most browsers have a free feature that can be enabled to block pop-up advertisements.

Use an account with limited permissions.

When navigating the web, it's a good security practice to use an account with limited permissions. If you do become infected, restricted permissions keep the malicious code from spreading and escalating to an administrative account.

Disable external media AutoRun and AutoPlay features.

Disabling AutoRun and AutoPlay features prevents external media infected with malicious code from automatically running on your computer.

Change your passwords.

If you believe your computer is infected, change your passwords. This includes any passwords for websites that may have been cached in your web browser. Create and use strong passwords, making them difficult for attackers to guess. (See Choosing and Protecting Passwords and Supplementing Passwords for more information.)

Keep software updated.

Install software patches on your computer so attackers do not take advantage of known vulnerabilities. Consider enabling automatic updates, when available. (See Understanding Patches and Software Updates for more information.)

Back up data.

Regularly back up your documents, photos, and important email messages to the cloud or to an external hard drive. In the event of an infection, your information will not be lost.

Install or enable a firewall.

Firewalls can prevent some types of infection by blocking malicious traffic before it enters your computer. Some operating systems include a firewall; if the operating system you are using includes one, enable it. (See Understanding Firewalls for Home and Small Office Use for more information.)

Use anti-spyware tools.

Spyware is a common virus source, but you can minimize infections by using a program that identifies and removes spyware. Most antivirus software includes an anti-spyware option; ensure you enable it.

Monitor accounts.

Look for any unauthorized use of, or unusual activity on, your accounts—especially banking accounts. If you identify unauthorized or unusual activity, contact your account provider immediately.

Avoid using public Wi-Fi.

Unsecured public Wi-Fi may allow an attacker to intercept your device's network traffic and gain access to your personal information.

What do you need to know about antivirus software?

Antivirus software scans computer files and memory for patterns that indicate the possible presence of malicious code. You can perform antivirus scans automatically or manually.

Automatic scans

Most antivirus software can scan specific files or directories automatically. New virus information is added frequently, so it is a good idea to take advantage of this option.

Manual scans

If your antivirus software does not automatically scan new files, you should manually scan files and media you receive from an outside source before opening them, including email attachments, web downloads, CDs, DVDs, and USBs.

Although anti-virus software can be a powerful tool in helping protect your computer, it can sometimes induce problems by interfering with the performance of your computer. Too much antivirus software can affect your computer's performance and the software's effectiveness.

Investigate your options in advance.

Research available antivirus and anti-spyware software to determine the best choice for you. Consider the amount of malicious code the software recognizes and how frequently the virus definitions are updated.

Also, check for known compatibility issues with other software you may be running on your computer.

Limit the number of programs you install.

Packages that incorporate both antivirus and anti-spyware capabilities together are now available. If you decide to choose separate programs, you only need one antivirus program and one anti-spyware program. Installing more programs increases your risk for problems.

There are many antivirus software program vendors, and deciding which one to choose can be confusing. Antivirus software programs all typically perform the same type of functions, so your decision may be based on recommendations, features, availability, or price. Regardless of which package you choose, installing any antivirus software will increase your level of protection.

How do you recover if you become a victim of malicious code?

Using antivirus software is the best way to defend your computer against malicious code. If you think your computer is infected, run your antivirus software program. Ideally, your antivirus program will identify any malicious code on your computer and quarantine them so they no longer affect your system. You should also consider these additional steps:

Minimize the damage.

If you are at work and have access to an information technology (IT) department, contact them immediately. The sooner they can investigate and "clean" your computer, the less likely it is to cause additional damage to your computer—and other computers on the network. If you are on a home computer or laptop, disconnect your computer from the internet; this will prevent the attacker from accessing your system.

Remove the malicious code.

If you have antivirus software installed on your computer, update the software and perform a manual scan of your entire system. If you do not have antivirus software, you can purchase it online or in a computer store. If the software cannot locate and remove the infection, you may need to reinstall your operating system, usually with a system restore disk. Note that reinstalling or restoring the operating system typically erases all of your files and any additional software that you have installed on your computer. After reinstalling the operating system and any other software, install all of the appropriate patches to fix known vulnerabilities.

Threats to your computer will continue to evolve. Although you cannot eliminate every hazard, by using caution, installing and using antivirus software, and following other simple security practices, you can significantly reduce your risk and strengthen your protection against malicious code.

INSPIRED? READY TO TAKE ACTION AND IMPLEMENT?

It's time to build your security culture anytime, anywhere, on any device. Not only do you get the tools and systems to become one of the most well-defended managed service providers around, you learn the mindset it takes to become successful in cybersecurity and can pass both on to your clients.

You'll also learn more about how you can assess, educate, and monitor your staff. There are hundreds of ways to improve your security based on your unique business. Now is the time to become competition and recession-proof.

Social Engineering

Using Instant Messaging and Chat Rooms Safely

Let's talk about Using Instant Messaging and Chat Rooms Safely.

Instant messaging and chat rooms offer an easy way to communicate with other people.

That said, there are dangers associated with tools that allow real-time communication.

What are the differences between some of the tools used for real-time communication?

Instant messaging or IM is often used for recreation.

IM is also becoming more widely used within corporations for communication between employees.

IM, regardless of the specific software you choose, provides a way for people to talk one-on-one.

Chat rooms

Whether public or private, chat rooms are forums for particular groups of people to interact.

Many chat rooms are based upon a shared characteristic.

For example, there are chat rooms for people of particular age groups or interests.

Most IM clients support "chats" among many users.

IM is traditionally one-to-one while chats are traditionally many-to-many.

Bots

A "chat robot," or "bot," is software that can interact with users through chat mechanisms, whether in IM or chat rooms.

In some cases, users may be able to get current weather reports, stock status, or movie listings.

In these instances, users are often aware that they are not interacting with an actual human.

But some users may be fooled by more sophisticated bots into thinking the responses they are receiving are from another person.

There are many software packages that incorporate one or more of these capabilities.

Many different technologies might be supported, including IM, Internet Relay Chat also known as "IRC" , or Jabber.

What are the dangers?

Identities can be elusive or ambiguous.

Not only is it sometimes difficult to identify whether the "person" you are talking to is human, but human nature and behavior isn't predictable.

People may lie about their identity, accounts may be compromised, users may forget to log out, or an account may be shared by many people.

These factors make it difficult to know who you're really talking to during a conversation.

Users are especially susceptible to certain types of attack.

Trying to convince someone to run a program or click on a link is a common attack method, but it can be especially effective through IM and chat rooms.

In a setting where a user feels comfortable with the "person" he or she is talking to, a malicious piece of software or an attacker has a better chance of convincing someone to fall into the trap.

You don't know who else might be seeing the conversation.

Online interactions are easy to save, and if you're using a free commercial service the exchanges may be archived on a server.

You have no control over what happens to those logs.

You also don't know if there's someone looking over the shoulder of the person you're talking to, or if an attacker might be "sniffing" your conversation.

The software you're using may contain vulnerabilities.

Like any other software, chat software may have vulnerabilities that attackers can exploit.

Default security settings may be inappropriate

The default security settings in chat software tend to be relatively permissive to make it more open and "usable," and this can make you more susceptible to attacks.

How can you use these tools safely?

Evaluate your security settings.

Check the default settings in your software and adjust them if they are too permissive.

Make sure to disable automatic downloads.

Some chat software offers the ability to limit interactions to only certain users, and you may want to take advantage of these restrictions.

Be conscious of what information you reveal.

Be wary of revealing personal information unless you know who you are really talking to.

You should also be careful about discussing anything you or your employer might consider sensitive business information over public IM or chat services.

This applies even if you're talking to someone you know in a one-to-one conversation.

Try to verify the identity of the person you are talking to, if it matters.

In some forums and situations, the identity of the "person" you are talking to may not matter.

If you need to have a degree of trust in that person, either because you are sharing certain types of information or being asked to take some action like following a link or running a program, make sure the "person" you are talking to is actually that person.

Don't believe everything you read.

The information or advice you receive in a chat room or by IM may be false or, worse, malicious.

Try to verify the information or instructions from outside sources before taking any action.

Keep software up to date.

This includes the chat software, your browser, your operating system, your mail client, and, especially, your anti-virus software.

Now you understand the basics of using instant messaging and chat rooms safely.

Real-World Warnings Keep You Safe Online

Let's talk about how Real-World Warnings Keep You Safe Online

Many of the warning phrases you probably heard from your parents and teachers are also applicable to using computers and the Internet.

Why are these warnings important?

Like the real world, technology and the Internet present dangers as well as benefits.

Equipment fails, attackers may target you, and mistakes and poor judgment happen.

Just as you take precautions to protect yourself in the real world, you need to take precautions to protect yourself online.

For many users, computers and the Internet are unfamiliar and intimidating, so it is appropriate to approach them the same way we urge children to approach the real world.

What are some warnings to remember?

Don't trust candy from strangers.

Finding something on the Internet does not guarantee that it is true.

Anyone can publish information online, so before accepting a statement as fact or taking action, verify that the source is reliable.

It is also easy for attackers to "spoof" email addresses, so verify that an email is legitimate before opening an unexpected email attachment or responding to a request for personal information.

If it sounds too good to be true, it probably is.

You have probably seen many emails promising fantastic rewards or monetary gifts.

However, regardless of what the email claims, there are not any wealthy strangers desperate to send you money.

Beware of grand promises.

They are most likely spam, hoaxes, or phishing schemes.

Also be wary of pop-up windows and advertisements for free downloadable software.

They may be disguising spyware.

Don't advertise that you are away from home

Some email accounts, especially within an organization, offer a feature (called an autoresponder) that allows you to create an "away" message if you are going to be away from your email for an extended period of time.

The message is automatically sent to anyone who emails you while the autoresponder is enabled.

While this is a helpful feature for letting your contacts know that you will not be able to respond right away, be careful how you phrase your message.

You do not want to let potential attackers know that you are not home, or, worse, give specific details about your location and itinerary.

Safer options include phrases such as "I will not have access to email between [date] and [date]."

If possible, also restrict the recipients of the message to people within your organization or in your address book.

If your away message replies to spam, it only confirms that your email account is active.

This practice may increase the amount of spam you receive.

Lock up your valuables

If an attacker is able to access your personal data, he or she may be able to compromise or steal the information.

Take steps to protect this information by following good security practices.

Some of the most basic precautions include:

1.   Locking your computer when you step away.
2.   Using firewalls, anti-virus software, and strong passwords.
3.   Installing appropriate software updates.
4.   And taking precautions when browsing or using email.

Have a backup plan

Since your information could be lost or compromised (due to an equipment malfunction, an error, or an attack), make regular backups of your information so that you still have clean, complete copies.

Backups also help you identify what has been changed or lost.

If your computer has been infected, it is important to remove the infection before resuming your work.

Keep in mind that if you did not realize that your computer was infected, your backups may also be compromised.

Now you know how to use real world warnings to keep yourself safe online.

Keeping Children Safe Online

Children present unique security risks when they use a computer—not only do you have to keep them safe, you have to protect the data on your computer. By taking some simple steps, you can dramatically reduce the threats.

What unique risks are associated with children?

When a child is using your computer, normal safeguards and security practices may not be sufficient. Children present additional challenges because of their natural characteristics: innocence, curiosity, desire for independence, and fear of punishment. You need to consider these characteristics when determining how to protect your data and the child.

You may think that because the child is only playing a game, or researching a term paper, or typing a homework assignment, they can't cause any harm.

But what if, when saving their paper, the child deletes a necessary program file? Or what if they unintentionally visit a malicious web page that infects your computer with a virus? These are just two possible scenarios.

Mistakes happen, but children may not realize what they've done or may not tell you what happened because they're afraid of getting punished.

Online predators present another significant threat, particularly to children. Because the nature of the internet is so anonymous, it is easy for people to misrepresent themselves and manipulate or trick other users (see Avoiding Social Engineering and Phishing Attacks for some examples).

Adults often fall victim to these ploys, and children, who are usually much more open and trusting, are even easier targets. Another growing problem is cyberbullying. These threats are even greater if a child has access to email or instant messaging programs, visits chat rooms, and/or uses social networking sites.

What can you do?

Be involved

Consider activities you can work on together, whether it be playing a game, researching a topic you had been talking about (e.g., family vacation spots, a particular hobby, a historical figure), or putting together a family newsletter. This will allow you to supervise your child's online activities while teaching them good computer habits.

Keep your computer in an open area

If your computer is in a high-traffic area, you will be able to easily monitor the computer activity. Not only does this accessibility deter children from doing something they know they're not allowed to do, it also gives you the opportunity to intervene if you notice a behavior that could have negative consequences.

Set rules and warn about dangers

Make sure your child knows the boundaries of what they are allowed to do on the computer. These boundaries should be appropriate for the child's age, knowledge, and maturity, but they may include rules about how long they are allowed to be on the computer, what sites they are allowed to visit, what software programs they can use, and what tasks or activities they are allowed to do.

You should also talk to children about the dangers of the internet so that they recognize suspicious behavior or activity.

Discuss the risks of sharing certain types of information (e.g., that they're home alone) and the benefits to only communicating and sharing information with people they know (see Using Instant Messaging and Chat Rooms Safely, Staying Safe on Social Network Sites, and the document Socializing Securely: Using Social Networking Services for more information).

The goal isn't to scare them, it's to make them more aware. Make sure to include the topic of cyberbullying in these discussions (see Dealing with Cyberbullies for more information).

Monitor computer activity

Be aware of what your child is doing on the computer, including which websites they are visiting. If they are using email, instant messaging, or chat rooms, try to get a sense of who they are corresponding with and whether they actually know them.

Keep lines of communication open

Let your child know that they can approach you with any questions or concerns about behaviors or problems they may have encountered on the computer.

Consider partitioning your computer into separate accounts

Most operating systems give you the option of creating a different user account for each user. If you're worried that your child may accidentally access, modify, and/or delete your files, you can give them a separate account and decrease the amount of access and number of privileges they have.

If you don't have separate accounts, you need to be especially careful about your security settings.

In addition to limiting functionality within your browser (see Evaluating Your Web Browser's Security Settings for more information), avoid letting your browser remember passwords and other personal information (see Browsing Safely: Understanding Active Content and Cookies).

Also, it is always important to keep your virus definitions up to date (see Understanding Anti-Virus Software).

Consider implementing parental controls

You may be able to set some parental controls within your browser. For example, Internet Explorer allows you to restrict or allow certain websites to be viewed on your computer, and you can protect these settings with a password.

To find those options, click **Tools** on your menu bar, select **Internet Options**, choose the **Content** tab, and click the **Enable...** button under **Content Advisor**.

There are other resources you can use to control and/or monitor your child's online activity. Some ISPs offer services designed to protect children online.

Contact your ISP to see if any of these services are available. There are also special software programs you can install on your computer. Different programs offer different features and capabilities, so you can find one that best suits your needs.

Dealing with Cyber Bullies

Bullies are taking advantage of technology to intimidate and harass their victims.

Dealing with cyberbullying can be difficult, but there are steps you can take.

What is cyberbullying?

Cyberbullying refers to practice of using technology to harass, or bully, someone else.

Bullies used to be restricted to methods such as physical intimidation, postal mail, or the telephone.

Now, developments in electronic media offer forums such as email, instant messaging, web pages, and digital photos to add to the arsenal.

Computers, cell phones, tablets, and other mobile devices are current tools that are being used to conduct an old practice.

Forms of cyberbullying can range in severity from cruel or embarrassing rumors to threats, harassment, or stalking.

It can affect any age group; however, teenagers and young adults are common victims, and cyberbullying is a growing problem in schools.

Why has cyberbullying become such a problem?

The relative anonymity of the internet is appealing for bullies because it enhances the intimidation and makes tracing the activity more difficult.

Some bullies also find it easier to be more vicious because there is no personal contact.

Unfortunately, the internet and email can also increase the visibility of the activity.

Information or pictures posted online or forwarded in mass emails can reach a larger audience faster than more traditional methods, causing more damage to the victims.

And because of the amount of personal information available online, bullies may be able to arbitrarily choose their victims.

Cyberbullying may also indicate a tendency toward more serious behavior.

While bullying has always been an unfortunate reality, most bullies grow out of it.

Cyberbullying has not existed long enough to have solid research, but there is evidence that it may be an early warning for more violent behavior.

How can you protect yourself or your children?

Teach your children good online habits.

Explain the risks of technology, and teach children how to be responsible online (see Keeping Children Safe Online for more information).

Reduce their risk of becoming cyberbullies by setting guidelines for and monitoring their use of the internet and other electronic media (cell phones, tablets, etc.).

Keep lines of communication open.

Regularly talk to your children about their online activities so that they feel comfortable telling you if they are being victimized.

Watch for warning signs.

If you notice changes in your child's behavior, try to identify the cause as soon as possible.

If cyberbullying is involved, acting early can limit the damage.

Limit availability of personal information.

Limiting the number of people who have access to contact information or details about interests, habits, or employment reduces exposure to bullies that you or your child do not know.

This may limit the risk of becoming a victim and may make it easier to identify the bully if you or your child are victimized.

Avoid escalating the situation.

Responding with hostility is likely to provoke a bully and escalate the situation.

Depending on the circumstances, consider ignoring the issue.

Often, bullies thrive on the reaction of their victims.

Other options include subtle actions.

For example, you may be able to block the messages on social networking sites or stop unwanted emails by changing the email address.

If you continue to get messages at the new email address, you may have a stronger case for legal action.

Document the activity.

Keep a record of any online activity (emails, web pages, instant messages, etc.), including relevant dates and times.

In addition to archiving an electronic version, consider printing a copy.

Report cyberbullying to the appropriate authorities.

If you or your child are being harassed or threatened, report the activity.

Many schools have instituted anti-bullying programs, so school officials may have established policies for dealing with activity that involves students.

If necessary, contact your local law enforcement.

Law enforcement agencies have different policies, but your local police department or FBI branch are good starting points.

Identifying Fake News, Hoaxes, and Urban Legends

Viral emails are familiar to anyone with an email account, whether they are sent by strangers or well-intentioned friends or family members. Try to verify the information before following any instructions or passing the message along.

Why are viral emails a problem?

Viral emails quickly propagate from person to person. Although they may seem harmless, these emails can contain malware or mask other malicious activity, which pose a serious risk to recipients.

Viral emails may not only make systems susceptible to malware, they may also

- Consume bandwidth or space within the recipient's inbox;
- Obligate people you know to waste time sifting through the messages and, in some cases, verifying the information; and
- Spread fear, uncertainty, and doubt.

What are some types of viral emails?

There are two main types of viral emails:

Hoaxes

Hoaxes attempt to trick or defraud recipients. A hoax could be malicious, e.g., instructing users to delete a file necessary to the operating system by claiming it is a virus. It could also be a scam that convinces users to send money or—in the case of a phishing attack—personal information (see Avoiding Social Engineering and Phishing Attacks for more information).

Urban legends

Viral emails that include urban legends usually warn of a threat and compel recipients to forward the email to others. These emails often pose as notifications of important or urgent information. Some viral emails containing urban legends may promise users monetary rewards for forwarding the message. Others may urge the recipient to sign a petition that the email claims will be submitted to a particular group.

How can you tell if the email is a hoax or urban legend?

Be especially cautious if the message has any of the characteristics listed below. **Note:** these characteristics are just guidelines—not every hoax or urban legend has these attributes, and legitimate messages may have some of these characteristics:

- It suggests tragic consequences for not performing some action.
- It promises money or gift certificates for performing some action.
- It offers instructions or attachments claiming to protect the recipient from a virus that is undetected by antivirus software.
- It claims it is not a hoax.
- It contains multiple spelling or grammatical errors, or the logic is contradictory.
- It contains a statement urging the recipient to forward the message.
- It has already been forwarded multiple times (evident from the trail of email headers in the body of the message).

If you want to check the validity of an email, there are websites that provide information about hoaxes and urban legends:

- Urban Legends and Folklore – http://urbanlegends.about.com/

- Urban Legends Reference Pages –
http://www.snopes.com/

Using Caution with USB Drives

USB drives are popular for storing and transporting data, but some of the characteristics that make them convenient also introduce security risks.

What security risks are associated with USB drives?

Because USB drives, sometimes known as thumb drives, are small, readily available, inexpensive, and extremely portable, they are popular for storing and transporting files from one computer to another.

However, these same characteristics make them appealing to attackers.

One option is for attackers to use your USB drive to infect other computers.

An attacker might infect a computer with malicious code, or malware, that can detect when a USB drive is plugged into a computer.

The malware then downloads malicious code onto the drive.

When the USB drive is plugged into another computer, the malware infects that computer.

Some attackers have also targeted electronic devices directly, infecting items such as electronic picture frames and USB drives during production.

When users buy the infected products and plug them into their computers, malware is installed on their computers.

Attackers may also use their USB drives to steal information directly from a computer.

If an attacker can physically access a computer, he or she can download sensitive information directly onto a USB drive.

Even computers that have been turned off may be vulnerable, because a computer's memory is still active for several minutes without power.

If an attacker can plug a USB drive into the computer during that time, he or she can quickly reboot the system from the USB drive and copy the computer's memory, including passwords, encryption keys, and other sensitive data, onto the drive.

Victims may not even realize that their computers were attacked.

The most obvious security risk for USB drives, though, is that they are easily lost or stolen.

Read Protecting Portable Devices: Physical Security for more information.

If the data was not backed up, the loss of a USB drive can mean hours of lost work and the potential that the information cannot be replicated.

And if the information on the drive is not encrypted, anyone who has the USB drive can access all of the data on it.

How can you protect your data?

There are steps you can take to protect the data on your USB drive and on any computer that you might plug the drive into:

Take advantage of security features.

Use passwords and encryption on your USB drive to protect your data, and make sure that you have the information backed up in case your drive is lost.

Read Protecting Portable Devices: Data Security for more information.

Keep personal and business USB drives separate.

Do not use personal USB drives on computers owned by your organization, and do not plug USB drives containing corporate information into your personal computer.

Use and maintain security software, and keep all software up to date.

Use a firewall, anti-virus software, and anti-spyware software to make your computer less vulnerable to attacks, and make sure to keep the virus definitions current.

Read Understanding Firewalls, Understanding Anti-Virus Software, and Recognizing and Avoiding Spyware for more information.

Also, keep the software on your computer up to date by applying any necessary patches.

Read Understanding Patches for more information.

Do not plug an unknown USB drive into your computer.

If you find a USB drive, give it to the appropriate authorities.

That may be a location's security personnel, your organization's IT department, etc.

Do not plug it into your computer to view the contents or to try to identify the owner.

Disable Autorun.

The Autorun feature causes removable media such as CDs, DVDs, and USB drives to open automatically when they are inserted into a drive.

By disabling Autorun, you can prevent malicious code on an infected USB drive from opening automatically.

In How to disable the Autorun functionality in Windows, Microsoft has provided a wizard to disable Autorun.

In the "More Information" section, look for the Microsoft® Fix it icon under the heading "How to disable or enable all Autorun features in Windows 7 and other operating systems."

INSPIRED? READY TO TAKE ACTION AND IMPLEMENT?

It's time to build your security culture anytime, anywhere, on any device. Not only do you get the tools and systems to become one of the most well-defended managed service providers around, you learn the

mindset it takes to become successful in cybersecurity and can pass both on to your clients.

You'll also learn more about how you can assess, educate, and monitor your staff. There are hundreds of ways to improve your security based on your unique business. Now is the time to become competition and recession-proof.

Visit www.HailBytes.com for free security resources!

Data Leakages

Don't collect personal information you don't need.

For example, the FTC's complaint against RockYou charged that the company collected lots of information during the site registration process, including the user's email address and email password. By collecting email passwords - not something the business needed - and then storing them in clear text, the FTC said the company created an unnecessary risk to people's email accounts. The business could have avoided that risk simply by not collecting sensitive information in the first place.

Safeguarding Your Data

It is especially important to take extra security precautions when multiple people use your computer—or when you store sensitive personal and work-related data on your computer.

Why isn't "more" better?

Maybe there is an extra software program included with a program you bought. Or perhaps you found a free download online. You may be tempted to install the programs just because you can, or because you think you might use them later.

However, even if the source and the software are legitimate, there may be hidden risks. And if other people use your computer, there are additional risks.

These risks become especially important if you use your computer to manage your personal finances (banking, taxes, online bill payment, etc.), store sensitive personal data, or perform work-related activities away from the office.

However, there are steps you can take to protect yourself.

How can you protect both your personal and work-related data?

Use and maintain anti-virus software and a firewall

Protect yourself against viruses and Trojan horses that may steal or modify the data on your own computer and leave you vulnerable by using anti-virus software and a firewall. (See Understanding Anti-Virus Software and Understanding Firewalls for more information.)

Make sure to keep your virus definitions up to date.

Regularly scan your computer for spyware

Spyware or adware hidden in software programs may affect the performance of your computer and give attackers access to your data.

Use a legitimate anti-spyware program to scan your computer and remove any of these files. (See

Recognizing and Avoiding Spyware for more information.) Many anti-virus products have incorporated spyware detection.

Keep software up to date

Install software patches so that attackers cannot take advantage of known problems or vulnerabilities. (See Understanding Patches for more information.) Many operating systems offer automatic updates. If this option is available, you should turn it on.

Evaluate your software's settings

The default settings of most software enable all available functionality. However, attackers may be able to take advantage of this functionality to access your computer. It is especially important to check the settings for software that connects to the internet (browsers, email clients, etc.). Apply the highest level of security available that still gives you the functionality you need.

Avoid unused software programs

Do not clutter your computer with unnecessary software programs. If you have programs on your computer that you do not use, consider uninstalling them. In addition to consuming system resources, these programs may contain vulnerabilities that, if not patched, may allow an attacker to access your computer.

Consider creating separate user accounts

If there are other people using your computer, you may be worried that someone else may accidentally access, modify, and/or delete your files. Most operating systems (including Windows XP and Vista, Mac OS X, and Linux) give you the option of creating a different user account for each user, and you can set the amount of access and privileges for each account.

You may also choose to have separate accounts for your work and personal purposes. While this approach will not completely isolate each area, it does offer some additional protection.

However, it will not protect your computer against vulnerabilities that give an attacker administrative privileges. Ideally, you will have separate computers for work and personal use; this will offer a different type of protection.

Establish guidelines for computer use

If there are multiple people using your computer, especially children, make sure they understand how to use the computer and internet safely. Setting boundaries and guidelines will help to protect your data. (See Keeping Children Safe Online for more information.)

Use passwords and encrypt sensitive files

Passwords and other security features add layers of protection if used appropriately. (See Choosing and Protecting Passwords and Supplementing Passwords for more information.) By encrypting files, you ensure that unauthorized people can't view data even if they can physically access it.

You may also want to consider options for full disk encryption, which prevents a thief from even starting your laptop without a passphrase. When you use encryption, it is important to remember your passwords and passphrases; if you forget or lose them, you may lose your data.

Follow corporate policies for handling and storing work-related information

If you use your computer for work-related purposes, make sure to follow any corporate policies for handling and storing the information.

These policies were likely established to protect proprietary information and customer data, as well as to protect you and the company from liability.

Even if it is not explicitly stated in your corporate policy, you should avoid allowing other people, including family members, to use a computer that contains corporate data.

Dispose of sensitive information properly

Simply deleting a file does not completely erase it. To ensure that an attacker cannot access these files, make sure that you adequately erase sensitive files. (See Effectively Erasing Files for more information.)

Follow good security habits

Review other security tips for ways to protect yourself and your data.

Proper Disposal of Electronic Devices

Dispose of sensitive data securely.

Paperwork or equipment you no longer need may look like trash, but it's treasure to identity thieves if it includes personal information about consumers or employees. For example, according to the FTC complaints in Rite Aid and CVS Caremark, the companies tossed sensitive personal information - like prescriptions - in dumpsters. In Goal FInancial, the FTC alleged that an employee sold surplus hard drives that contained the sensitive personal information of approximately 34,000 customers in clear text. The companies could have prevented the risk to consumers' personal information by shredding, burning, or pulverizing documents to make them unreadable and by using available technology to wipe devices that aren't in use.

Why is it important to dispose of electronic devices safely?

In addition to effectively securing sensitive information on electronic devices, it is important to follow best practices for electronic device disposal.

Computers, smartphones, and cameras allow you to keep a great deal of information at your fingertips, but when you dispose of, donate, or recycle a device you may inadvertently disclose sensitive information which could be exploited by cyber criminals.

Types of electronic devices include:

Computers, smartphones, and tablets

Electronic devices that can automatically store and process data; most contain a central processing unit and memory, and use an operating system that runs programs and applications.

Digital media

These electronic devices create, store, and play digital content. Digital media devices include items like digital cameras and media players.

External hardware and peripheral devices

Hardware devices that provide input and output for computers, such as printers, monitors, and external hard drives; these devices contain permanently stored digital characters.

Gaming consoles

Electronic, digital, or computer devices that output a video signal or visual image to display a video game.

What are some effective methods for removing data from your device?

Hold on to information only as long as you have a legitimate business need.

In the FTC's BJ's Wholesale Club case, the company collected customer's credit and debit card information to process transactions in its retail stores. But according to the complaint, it continued to store that data for up to 30 days - long after the sale was complete. Not only did that violate bank rules, but by holding on to the information without a legitimate business need, the FTC said BJ's Wholesale Club created an unreasonable risk. By exploiting other weaknesses in the company's security practices, hackers stole the account data and used it to make counterfeit credit and debit cards. The business could have limited its risk by securely disposing of the financial information once it no longer had a legitimate need for it.

There are a variety of methods for permanently erasing data from your devices (also called sanitizing). Because methods of sanitization vary according to device, it is important to use the method that applies to that particular device.

Methods for sanitization include:

Backing up data.

Saving your data to another device or a second location (e.g., an external hard drive or the cloud) can help you recover your data if your device is stolen.

Options for digital storage include cloud data services, CDs, DVDs, and removable flash drives or removable hard drives (see Using Caution with USB Drives and Protecting Portable Devices: Data Security for more information).

Backing up your data can also help you identify exactly what information a thief may have been able to access.

Deleting data.

Removing data from your device can be one method of sanitization. When you delete files from a device—although the files may appear to have been removed—data remains on the media even after a delete or format command is executed.

Do not rely solely on the deletion method you routinely use, such as moving a file to the trash or recycle bin or selecting "delete" from the menu.

Even if you empty the trash, the deleted files are still on device and can be retrieved. Permanent data deletion requires several steps.

Computers.

Use a disk cleaning software designed to permanently remove the data stored on a computer hard drive to prevent the possibility of recovery.

Secure erase. This is a set of commands in the firmware of most computer hard drives. If you select a program that runs the secure erase command set, it will erase the data by overwriting all areas of the hard drive.

Disk wiping. This is a utility that erases sensitive information on hard drives and securely wipes flash drives and secure digital cards.

Smartphones and tablets.

Ensure that all data is removed from your device by performing a "hard reset." This will return the device to its original factory settings.

Each device has a different hard reset procedure, but most smartphones and tablets can be reset through their settings.

In addition, physically remove the memory card and the subscriber identity module card, if your device has one.

Digital cameras, media players, and gaming consoles.

Perform a standard factory reset (i.e., a hard reset) and physically remove the hard drive or memory card.

Office equipment (e.g., copiers, printers, fax machines, multifunction devices).

Remove any memory cards from the equipment. Perform a full manufacture reset to restore the equipment to its factory default.

Overwriting.

Another method of sanitization is to delete sensitive information and write new binary data over it.

Using random data instead of easily identifiable patterns makes it harder for attackers to discover the original information underneath. Since data stored on a computer is written in binary code—strings of 0s and 1s—one method of overwriting is to zero-fill a hard disk and select programs that use all zeros in the last layer.

Users should overwrite the entire hard disk and add multiple layers of new data (three to seven passes of new binary data) to prevent attackers from obtaining the original data.

Cipher.exe is a built-in command-line tool in Microsoft Windows operating systems that can be used to encrypt or decrypt data on New Technology File System drives. This tool also securely deletes data by overwriting it.

Clearing is a level of media sanitation that does not allow information to be retrieved by data, disk, or file recovery utilities. The National Institute of Standards and Technology (NIST) notes that devices must be resistant to keystroke recovery attempts from standard input devices (e.g., a keyboard or mouse) and from data scavenging tools.

Destroying.

Physical destruction of a device is the ultimate way to prevent others from retrieving your information.

Specialized services are available that will disintegrate, burn, melt, or pulverize your computer drive and other devices. These sanitization methods are designed to completely destroy the media and are typically carried out at an outsourced metal destruction or licensed incineration facility.

If you choose not to use a service, you can destroy your hard drive by driving nails or drilling holes into the device yourself. The remaining physical pieces of the drive must be small enough (at least 1/125 inches) that your information cannot be reconstructed from them. There are also hardware devices available that erase CDs and DVDs by destroying their surface.

Magnetic media degaussers.

Degaussers expose devices to strong magnetic fields that remove the data that is magnetically stored on traditional magnetic media.

Solid-state destruction.

The destruction of all data storage chip memory by crushing, shredding, or disintegration is called solid-state destruction. Solid-State Drives should be destroyed with devices that are specifically engineered for this purpose.

CD and DVD destruction.

Many office and home paper shredders can shred CDs and DVDs (be sure to check that the shredder you are using can shred CDs and DVDs before attempting this method).

For more information, see the NIST Special Publication 800-88 Guidelines for Media Sanitization.

How can you safely dispose of out-of-date electronic devices?

Electronic waste (sometimes called e-waste) is a term used to describe electronics that are nearing the end of their useful life and are discarded, donated, or recycled.

Although donating and recycling electronic devices conserves natural resources, you may still choose to dispose of e-waste by contacting your local landfill and requesting a designated e-waste drop off location.

Be aware that although there are many options for disposal, it is your responsibility to ensure that the location chosen is reputable and certified.

Effectively Erasing Files

Securely store sensitive files.

If it's necessary to retain important paperwork, take steps to keep it secure. In the Gregory Navone case, the FTC alleged that the defendant maintained sensitive consumer information, collected by his former businesses, in boxes in his garage. In Lifelock, the complaint charged that the company left faxed documents that included consumers' personal information in an open and easily accessible area. In each case, the business could have reduced the risk to their customers by implementing policies to store documents securely.

Before selling or discarding an old computer, or throwing away a CD or DVD, you naturally make sure that you've copied all of the files you need.

You've probably also attempted to delete your personal files so that other people aren't able to access them. However, unless you have taken the proper steps to make sure the hard drive, CD, or DVD is erased, people may still be able to resurrect those files.

Where do deleted files go?

When you delete a file, depending on your operating system and your settings, it may be transferred to your trash or recycle bin.

This "holding area" essentially protects you from yourself—if you accidentally delete a file, you can easily restore it. However, you may have experienced the panic that results from emptying the trash bin prematurely or having a file seem to disappear on its own.

The good news is that even though it may be difficult to locate, the file is probably still somewhere on your machine. The bad news is that even though you think you've deleted a file, an attacker or other unauthorized person may be able to retrieve it.

What are the risks?

Think of the information you have saved on your computer.

Is there banking or credit card account information? Tax returns? Passwords? Medical or other personal data? Personal photos? Sensitive corporate information? How much would someone be able to find out about you or your company by looking through your computer files?

Depending on what kind of information an attacker can find, he or she may be able to use it maliciously. You may become a victim of identity theft. Another possibility is that the information could be used in a social engineering attack.

Attackers may use information they find about you or an organization you're affiliated with to appear to be legitimate and gain access to sensitive data (see Avoiding Social Engineering and Phishing Attacks for more information).

Can you erase files by reformatting?

Reformatting your hard drive, CD, or DVD may superficially delete the files, but the information is still buried somewhere. Unless those areas of the disk are effectively overwritten with new content, it is still possible that knowledgeable attackers may be able to access the information.

How can you be sure that your information is completely erased?

Some people use extreme measures to make sure their information is destroyed, but these measures can be dangerous and may not be completely successful.

Your best option is to investigate software programs and hardware devices that claim to erase your hard drive, CD, or DVD.

Even so, these programs and devices have varying levels of effectiveness. When choosing a software program to perform this task, look for the following characteristics:

"Secure Erase" is performed

Secure Erase is a standard in modern hard drives. If you select a program that runs the Secure Erase command, it will erase data by overwriting all areas of the hard drive, even areas that are not being used.

Data is written multiple times

It is important to make sure that not only is the information erased, but new data is written over it. By adding multiple layers of data, the program makes it difficult for an attacker to "peel away" the new layer. Three to seven passes is fairly standard and should be sufficient.

Random data is used

Using random data instead of easily identifiable patterns makes it harder for attackers to determine the

---

pattern and discover the original information underneath.

Zeros are used in the final layer

Regardless of how many times the program overwrites the data, look for programs that use all zeros in the last layer. This adds an additional level of security.

While many of these programs assume that you want to erase an entire disk, there are programs that give you the option to erase and overwrite individual files.

An effective way to ruin a CD or DVD is to wrap it in a paper towel and shatter it. However, there are also hardware devices that erase CDs or DVDs by destroying their surface. Some of these devices actually shred the media itself, while others puncture the writable surface with a pattern of holes.

Many paper shredders will also shred CDs and DVDs. If you decide to use one of these devices, compare the various features and prices to determine which option best suits your needs.

INSPIRED? READY TO TAKE ACTION AND IMPLEMENT?

It's time to build your security culture anytime, anywhere, on any device. Not only do you get the tools and systems to become one of the most well-defended managed service providers around, you learn the mindset it takes to become successful in cybersecurity and can pass both on to your clients.

You'll also learn more about how you can assess, educate, and monitor your staff. There are hundreds of ways to improve your security based on your unique business. Now is the time to become competition and recession-proof.

Visit www.HailBytes.com for free security resources!

Passwords & Security Questions

Insist on complex and unique passwords.

"Passwords like 121212 or qwerty aren't much better than no passwords at all. THat's why it's wise to give some thought to the password standards you implement. In the Twitter case, for example, the company let employees use common

dictionary words as administrative passwords, as well as passwords they were already using for other accounts. According to the FTC, those lax practices left Twitter's system vulnerable to hackers who used password-guessing tools, or tried passwords stolen from other services in the hope that Twitter employees used the same password to access the company's system. Twitter could have limited those risks by implementing a more secure password system -- for example, by requiring employees to choose complex passwords and training them not to use the same or similar passwords for both business and personal accounts.

Choosing and Protecting Passwords

Passwords are a common form of authentication and are often the only barrier between you and your personal information.

There are several programs attackers can use to help guess or "crack" passwords.

But if you choose good passwords and keep them confidential, you can make it more difficult for an unauthorized person to access your information.

Why do you need strong passwords?

You probably use a number of personal identification numbers (PINs), passwords, and passphrases every day: from getting money from the ATM or using your debit card in a store, to logging in to your email or into an online retailer.

Keeping track of all of the number, letter, and word combinations may be frustrating at times, but you've seen enough news coverage to know that hackers represent a real threat to your information.

Often, an attack is not specifically about your account, but about using the access to your information to launch a larger attack.

One of the best ways to protect information or physical property is to ensure that only authorized people have access to it.

Verifying that those requesting access are the people they claim to be is the next step.

This authentication process is more important and more difficult in the cyber world.

Passwords are the most common means of authentication, but only work if they are complex and confidential.

Many systems and services have been successfully breached because of insecure and inadequate passwords.

Once a system is compromised, it's open to exploitation by other unwanted sources.

How can you choose good passwords?

Avoid common mistakes

Most people use passwords that are based on personal information and are easy to remember.

However, that also makes it easier for an attacker to crack them.

Consider a four-digit PIN.

Is yours a combination of the month, day, or year of your birthday?

Does it contain your address or phone number?

Think about how easy it is to find someone's birthday or similar information.

What about your email password—is it a word that can be found in the dictionary?

If so, it may be susceptible to dictionary attacks, which attempt to guess passwords based on common words or phrases.

Although intentionally misspelling a word ("daytt" instead of "date") may offer some protection against dictionary attacks, an even better method is to rely on a series of words and use memory techniques, or mnemonics, to help you remember how to decode it.

For example, instead of the password "hoops," use "IITpbb" for "[I] [l]ike [T]o [p]lay [b]asket[b]all."

Using both lowercase and capital letters adds another layer of obscurity.

Changing the same example used above to "Il!2pBb." creates a password very different from any dictionary word.

Length and complexity

The National Institute of Standards and Technology (NIST) has developed specific guidelines for strong passwords.

According to NIST guidance, you should consider using the longest password or passphrase permissible (8–64 characters) when you can.

For example, "Pattern2baseball#4mYmiemale!" would be a strong password because it has 28 characters.

It also includes the upper and lowercase letters, numbers, and special characters.

You may need to try different variations of a passphrase—some applications limit the length of passwords, some do not accept spaces or certain special characters.

Avoid common phrases, famous quotations, and song lyrics.

Dos and don'ts

Once you've come up with a strong, memorable password it's tempting to reuse it – don't!

Reusing a password, even a strong one, endangers your accounts just as much as using a weak password.

If attackers guess your password, they would have access to all of your accounts.

Use the following techniques to develop unique passwords for each of your accounts:

Do use different passwords on different systems and accounts.

Don't use passwords that are based on personal information that can be easily accessed or guessed.

Do use the longest password or passphrase permissible by each password system

Don't use words that can be found in any dictionary of any language.

Do develop mnemonics to remember complex passwords.

Do consider using a password manager program to keep track of your passwords. (See more information below.)

How to protect your passwords

Store passwords securely.

Don't make it easy for interlopers to access passwords. In Guidance Software, the FTC alleged that the company stored network user credentials in clear, readable text that helped a hacker access customer credit card information on the network. Similarly, in Reed Elsevier, the FTC charged that the business allowed customers to store user credentials in a vulnerable format in cookies on their computers. In Twitter, too, the FTC said the company failed to establish policies that prohibited employees from storing administrative passwords in plain text in personal email accounts. In each of those cases, the risks could have been reduced if the companies had policies and procedures in place to store credentials securely. Businesses also may want to consider other protections - two-factor authentication, for example - that can help protect against password compromises.

Now that you've chosen a password that's easy for you to remember, but difficult for others to guess, you have to make sure not to leave it someplace for people to find.

Writing it down and leaving it in your desk, next to your computer, or, worse, taped to your computer, is just making it easy for someone who has physical access to your office.

 Don't tell anyone your passwords, and watch for attackers trying to trick you through phone calls or email messages requesting that you reveal your passwords.

Read Avoiding Social Engineering and Phishing Attacks for more information.

Programs called password managers offer the option to create randomly generated passwords for all of your accounts.

You then access those strong passwords with a master password.

If you use a password manager, remember to use a strong master password.

Password problems can stem from your web browsers' ability to save passwords and your online sessions in memory.

Depending on your web browsers' settings, anyone with access to your computer may be able to discover all of your passwords and gain access to your information.

Always remember to log out when you are using a public computer (at the library, an Internet cafe, or even a shared computer at your office).

Avoid using public computers and public Wi-Fi to access sensitive accounts such as banking and email.

There's no guarantee that these techniques will prevent an attacker from learning your password, but they will make it more difficult.

For more information on passwords, multi-factor authentication, and related password topics, Read Supplementing Passwords.

Don't forget security basics:

Keep your operating system, browser, and other software up-to-date.

Use and maintain anti-virus software and a firewall.

Read Understanding Anti-Virus Software and Understanding Firewalls.

Regularly scan your computer for spyware.

Some anti-virus programs incorporate spyware detection.

Use caution with email attachments and untrusted links.

Watch for suspicious activity on your accounts.

Supplementing Passwords

Passwords are a common form of protecting information, but passwords alone may not provide adequate security.

For the best protection, look for sites that have additional ways to verify your identity.

Why aren't passwords sufficient?

Passwords are a good first layer of protection, but attackers can guess or intercept passwords.

Additional security measures can protect you even if an attacker does obtain your password.

You can strengthen that first layer of protection by avoiding passwords based on personal information;

using the longest password or passphrase possible (8–64 characters); and not sharing your passwords with anyone else.

ReadChoosing and Protecting Passwords for more information.

What additional levels of security are available?

Multi-factor authentication, simultaneously using multiple pieces of information to verify your identity, is becoming more common.

You may see multi-factor authentication, or MFA, advertised as two-factor authentication or 2FA.

Even if an attacker obtains your password, he may not be able to access your account if it's protected by MFA.

The theory behind this approach is similar to requiring two or more forms of identification or two keys to open a safe deposit box.

You should turn on MFA where it's available.

Authentication categories include

Something you know, typically answers to secret questions or passwords.

Something you have such as a token or other item in your possession.

And **something you are** like a biometric measure such as a fingerprint, face, or eye scan.

Something you know.

This includes passwords or pre-established answers to questions.

We'll cover tips below for setting up good answers to these "secret questions."

Something you have.

This could be a small physical token such as a smart card, a special key fob, or USB drive.

You might use this token in conjunction with a password to log into an account.

However, software-based tokens are also common.

These software-based tokens can generate a single-use login personal identification number (PIN).

Other variations include SMS messages, phone calls, or emails sent to the user with a verification PIN.

These token PINs can often be used only once and are voided immediately after use.

So, even if an attacker intercepts the exchange, the attacker will not be able to use the information again to access your account.

Something you are.

Biometric identification can include scanning of eyes (retinas or irises) or fingerprints, other facial recognition, voice recognition, or authentication through signatures or keystroke movements.

A common example of biometric identification is the fingerprint scanner used to sign in users on many modern smartphones.

Another form of verification is the use of **personal web certificates.**

Unlike certificates used to identify web sites, which we cover in "Understanding Web Site Certificates", personal web certificates are used to identify individual users.

A website using personal web certificates relies on these certificates and the authentication process of the corresponding public/private keys to verify that you are who you claim to be.

We cover this in more depth in Understanding Digital Signatures and Understanding Encryption.

Because information identifying you is embedded within the certificate, an additional password is unnecessary.

However, you should have a password to protect your private key so that attackers can't gain access to your key and represent themselves as you.

This process is similar to MFA, but it differs in this way: the password protecting your private key is used to decrypt the information on your computer and is never sent over the network.

What other measures keep your passwords secure?

Guard against brute force attacks.

Remember that adage about an infinite number of monkeys at an infinite number of typewriters? Hackers use automated programs that perform a similar function. These brute force attacks work by typing endless combinations of characters until hackers luck into someone's password. In the Lookout Services, Twitter, and Reed Elsevier cases, the FTC alleged that the businesses didn't suspend or disable user credentials after a certain number of unsuccessful login attempts. By not adequately restricting the number of tries, the companies placed their networks at risk. Implementing a policy to suspend or disable accounts after repeated login attempts would have helped to eliminate that risk.

IT security professionals and administrators should implement the following security measures to help further protect passwords:

"Salt and hash" passwords.

Salting is the addition of unique, random characters to the password before it is hashed.

The salt value should be no less than 32 bits in length.

Hashing is the process of scrambling a password using a set algorithm.

Use strong authentication recovery mechanisms.

Weak authentication recovery mechanisms can be misused to allow an attacker to gain unauthorized access to an affected system.

Strong mechanisms prevent unauthorized access to an account or to reset the user's password.

Implement an account lockout policy.

Account lockout should initiate after a pre-defined number of failed attempts.

Set accounts to automatically disable.

Accounts should be disabled after being inactive for a predefined amount of time.

What if you lose your password or certificate?

Perhaps you've forgotten your password or you've reformatted your computer and lost your personal web certificate.

Most organizations have procedures for giving you access to your information in these situations.

For the best security, keep information on your account up to date.

This includes alternate email addresses or phone numbers that can help verify your identity if you forget your password.

In the case of certificates, you may need to request that the organization issue you a new one.

In the case of passwords, you may just need a reminder.

No matter what happened, the organization needs a way to verify your identity.

To do this, many organizations rely on **secret questions**.

When you open a new account (e.g., email, credit card), some organizations will prompt you to provide them with the answer to a question.

They may ask you this question if you forget your password or request information about your account over the phone.

If your answer matches the answer they have on file, they will assume that they are actually communicating with you.

In theory, secret questions and answers can protect your information.

However, common secret questions ask for mother's maiden name, social security number, date of birth, or your pet's name.

Because so much personal information is now available online or through other public sources, attackers may be able to discover the answers to these questions.

Realize that the secret question is really just an additional password.

When establishing the answer, you don't have to supply real information.

In fact, if you're asked to provide a pre-established answer, dishonesty may be the best policy.

Choose your answer as you would choose any other good password, store it in a secure location, like in a password manager, and don't share it with other people.

While additional security practices offer you more protection than a password alone, they should not be considered completely effective.

Increasing the level of security only makes it more difficult for attackers to access your information.

Be aware of MFA and other security practices when choosing a bank, credit card company, or other organization that will have access to your personal information.

Don't be afraid to ask what kind of security practices the organization uses.

INSPIRED? READY TO TAKE ACTION AND IMPLEMENT?

It's time to build your security culture anytime, anywhere, on any device. Not only do you get the tools and systems to become one of the most well-defended managed service providers around, you learn the mindset it takes to become successful in cybersecurity and can pass both on to your clients.

You'll also learn more about how you can assess, educate, and monitor your staff. There are hundreds of ways to improve your security based on your unique business. Now is the time to become competition and recession-proof.

Visit www.HailBytes.com for free security resources!

Safe Browsing

How Anonymous Are You?

You may think that you are anonymous as you browse websites, but pieces of information about you are always left behind. You can reduce the amount of information revealed about you by visiting legitimate sites, checking privacy policies, and minimizing the amount of personal information you provide.

What information is collected?

When you visit a website, a certain amount of information is automatically sent to the site. This information may include the following:

IP address

Each computer on the internet is assigned a specific, unique IP (internet protocol) address. Your computer may have a static IP address or a dynamic IP address. If you have a static IP address, it never changes. However, some ISPs own a block of addresses and assign an open one each time you connect to the internet—this is a dynamic IP address. You can determine your computer's IP address at any given time by visiting www.showmyip.com.

Domain name

The internet is divided into domains, and every user's account is associated with one of those domains. You can identify the domain by looking at the end of URL; for example, .edu indicates an educational institution, .gov indicates a US government agency, .org refers to organization, and .com is for commercial use. Many countries also have specific domain names. The list of active domain names is available from the Internet Assigned Numbers Authority (IANA).

Software details

It may be possible for an organization to determine which browser, including the version, that you used to access its site. The organization may also be able to determine what operating system your computer is running.

Page visits

Information about which pages you visited, how long you stayed on a given page, and whether you came to the site from a search engine is often available to the organization operating the website.

If a website uses cookies, the organization may be able to collect even more information, such as your browsing patterns, which include other sites you've visited. If the site you're visiting is malicious, files on your computer, as well as passwords stored in the temporary memory, may be at risk.

How is this information used?

Generally, organizations use the information that is gathered automatically for legitimate purposes, such as generating statistics about their sites. By analyzing the statistics, the organizations can better understand the popularity of the site and which areas of content are being accessed the most.

They may be able to use this information to modify the site to better support the behavior of the people visiting it.

Another way to apply information gathered about users is marketing. If the site uses cookies to determine other sites or pages you have visited, it may use this information to advertise certain products. The products may be on the same site or may be offered by partner sites.

However, some sites may collect your information for malicious purposes. If attackers are able to access files, passwords, or personal information on your computer, they may be able to use this data to their advantage.

The attackers may be able to steal your identity, using and abusing your personal information for financial gain. A common practice is for attackers to use this type of information once or twice, then sell or trade it to other people.

The attackers profit from the sale or trade, and increasing the number of transactions makes it more difficult to trace any activity back to them. The attackers may also alter the security settings on your computer so that they can access and use your computer for other malicious activity.

Are you exposing any other personal information?

While using cookies may be one method for gathering information, the easiest way for attackers to get access to personal information is to ask for it. By representing a malicious site as a legitimate one, attackers may be able to convince you to give them your address, credit card information, social security number, or other personal data (see Avoiding Social Engineering and Phishing Attacks for more information).

How can you limit the amount of information collected about you?

Be careful supplying personal information

Unless you trust a site, don't give your address, password, or credit card information. Look for indications that the site uses SSL to encrypt your information (see Protecting Your Privacy for more information). Although some sites require you to supply your social security number (e.g., sites associated with financial transactions such as loans or credit cards), be especially wary of providing this information online.

Limit cookies

If an attacker can access your computer, he or she may be able to find personal data stored in cookies. You may not realize the extent of the information stored on your computer until it is too late. However, you can limit the use of cookies (see Browsing Safely: Understanding Active Content and Cookies for more information).

Browse safely

Be careful which websites you visit; if it seems suspicious, leave the site. Also make sure to take precautions by increasing your security settings (see Evaluating Your Web Browser's Security Settings for more information), keeping your virus definitions up to date (see Understanding Anti-Virus Software for more information), and scanning your computer for spyware (see Recognizing and Avoiding Spyware for more information).

Staying Safe on Social Networking Sites

The popularity of social networking sites continues to increase, especially among teenagers and young adults.

The nature of these sites introduces security risks, so you should take certain precautions.

What are social networking sites?

Social networking sites, sometimes referred to as "friend-of-a-friend" sites, build upon the concept of traditional social networks where you are connected to new people through people you already know.

The purpose of some networking sites may be purely social, allowing users to establish friendships or romantic relationships, while others may focus on establishing business connections.

Although the features of social networking sites differ, they all allow you to provide information about yourself and offer some type of communication mechanism.

This is usually forums, chat rooms, email, or instant messages that enable you to connect with other users.

On some sites, you can browse for people based on certain criteria, while other sites require that you be "introduced" to new people through a connection you share.

Many of the sites have communities or subgroups that may be based on a particular interest.

What security implications do these sites present?

Social networking sites rely on connections and communication, so they encourage you to provide a certain amount of personal information.

When deciding how much information to reveal, people may not exercise the same amount of caution as they would when meeting someone in person because the internet provides a sense of anonymity.

The lack of physical interaction provides a false sense of security.

People tend to tailor the information for their friends to read, forgetting that others may see it.

Often they want to offer insights to impress potential friends or associates.

While the majority of people using these sites do not pose a threat, malicious people may be drawn to them because of the accessibility and amount of personal information that's available.

The more information malicious people have about you, the easier it's for them to take advantage of you.

Predators may form relationships online and then convince unsuspecting individuals to meet them in person.

That could lead to a dangerous situation.

The personal information can also be used to conduct a social engineering attack.

Using information that you provide about your location, hobbies, interests, and friends, a malicious person could impersonate a trusted friend or convince you that they have the authority to access other personal or financial data.

Additionally, because of the popularity of these sites, attackers may use them to distribute malicious code.

Sites that offer applications developed by third parties are particularly susceptible.

Attackers may be able to create customized applications that appear to be innocent while infecting your computer or sharing your information without your knowledge.

How can you protect yourself?

Limit the amount of personal information you post.

Don't post information that would make you vulnerable, such as your address or information about your schedule or routine.

If your connections post information about you, make sure the combined information is not more than you would be comfortable with strangers knowing.

Also be considerate when posting information, including photos, about your connections.

Remember that the internet is a public resource.

Only post information you are comfortable with anyone seeing.

This includes information and photos in your profile and in blogs and other forums.

Also, once you post information online, you can't retract it.

Even if you remove the information from a site, saved or cached versions may still exist on other people's machines.

Be wary of strangers.

The internet makes it easy for people to misrepresent their identities and motives.

Consider limiting the people who are allowed to contact you on these sites.

If you interact with people you do not know, be cautious about the amount of information you reveal or agreeing to meet them in person.

Be skeptical.

Don't believe everything you read online.

People may post false or misleading information about various topics, including their own identities.

This is not necessarily done with malicious intent; it could be unintentional, an exaggeration, or a joke.

Take appropriate precautions, though, and try to verify the authenticity of any information before taking any action.

Evaluate your settings.

Take advantage of a site's privacy settings.

The default settings for some sites may allow anyone to see your profile, but you can customize your settings to restrict access to only certain people.

There's still a risk that private information could be exposed despite these restrictions, so don't post anything that you wouldn't want the public to see.

Sites may change their options periodically, so review your security and privacy settings regularly to make sure that your choices are still appropriate.

Be wary of third-party applications.

Third-party applications may provide entertainment or functionality, but use caution when deciding which applications to enable.

Avoid applications that seem suspicious, and modify your settings to limit the amount of information the applications can access.

Use strong passwords.

Protect your account with passwords that cannot easily be guessed.

If your password is compromised, someone else may be able to access your account and pretend to be you.

Check privacy policies.

Some sites may share information such as email addresses or user preferences with other companies.

This may lead to an increase in spam.

Also, try to locate the policy for handling referrals to make sure that you do not unintentionally sign your friends up for spam.

Some sites will continue to send email messages to anyone you refer until they join.

Keep software, particularly your web browser, up to date.

Install software updates so that attackers cannot take advantage of known problems or vulnerabilities.

Many operating systems offer automatic updates.

If this option is available, you should enable it.

Use and maintain anti-virus software

Anti-virus software helps protect your computer against known viruses, so you may be able to detect and remove the virus before it can do any damage.

Because attackers are continually writing new viruses, it's important to keep your definitions up to date.

Children are especially susceptible to the threats that social networking sites present.

Although many of these sites have age restrictions, children may misrepresent their ages so that they can join.

 By teaching children about Internet safety, being aware of their online habits, and guiding them to appropriate sites, parents can make sure that the children become safe and responsible users.

Shopping Safely Online

Online shopping has become a popular way to purchase items without the hassles of traffic and crowds. However, the internet has unique risks, so it is

---

important to take steps to protect yourself when shopping online.

Why do online shoppers have to take special precautions?

The internet offers convenience not available from other shopping outlets. From the comfort of your home, you can search for items from multiple vendors, compare prices with a few mouse clicks, and make purchases without waiting in line.

However, the internet is also convenient for attackers, giving them multiple ways to access the personal and financial information of unsuspecting shoppers.

Attackers who are able to obtain this information may use it for their own financial gain, either by making purchases themselves or by selling the information to someone else.

How do attackers target online shoppers?

There are three common ways that attackers can take advantage of online shoppers:

Creating fraudulent sites and email messages

Unlike traditional shopping, where you know that a store is actually the store it claims to be, attackers can create malicious websites or email messages that appear to be legitimate. Attackers may also misrepresent themselves as charities, especially after natural disasters or during holiday seasons.

Attackers create these malicious sites and email messages to try to convince you to supply personal and financial information.

Intercepting insecure transactions

If a vendor does not use encryption, an attacker may be able to intercept your information as it is transmitted.

Targeting vulnerable computers

If you do not take steps to protect your computer from viruses or other malicious code, an attacker may be able to gain access to your computer and all of the information on it. It is also important for vendors to protect their computers to prevent attackers from accessing customer databases.

How can you protect yourself?

Do business with reputable vendors

Before providing any personal or financial information, make sure that you are interacting with a reputable, established vendor. Some attackers may try to trick you by creating malicious websites that appear to be legitimate, so you should verify the legitimacy before supplying any information. (See Avoiding Social Engineering and Phishing Attacks and Understanding Web Site Certificates for more information.)

Attackers may obtain a site certificate for a malicious website to appear more authentic, so review the certificate information, particularly the "issued to" information. Locate and note phone numbers and physical addresses of vendors in case there is a problem with your transaction or your bill.

Make sure your information is being encrypted

Many sites use secure sockets layer to encrypt information. Indications that your information will be encrypted include a Uniform Resource Locator that begins with "https:" instead of "http:" and a padlock icon. If the padlock is closed, the information is encrypted. The location of the icon varies by browser; for example, it may be to the right of the address bar or at the bottom of the window. Some attackers try to trick users by adding a fake padlock icon, so make sure that the icon is in the appropriate location for your browser.

Be wary of emails requesting information

Attackers may attempt to gather information by sending emails requesting that you confirm purchase or account information. (See Avoiding Social Engineering and Phishing Attacks.) Legitimate businesses will not solicit this type of information through email. Do not provide sensitive information through email. If you receive an unsolicited email from a business, instead of clicking on the provided link, directly log on to the authentic website by typing the address yourself. (See Recognizing and Avoiding Email Scams.)

Use a credit card

There are laws to limit your liability for fraudulent credit card charges, but you may not have the same level of protection for your debit cards. Additionally, because a debit card draws money directly from your bank account, unauthorized charges could leave you with insufficient funds to pay other bills. You can minimize potential damage by using a single, low-limit credit card to make all of your online purchases. Also use a credit card when using a payment gateway such as PayPal, Google Wallet, or Apple Pay.

Check your shopping app settings

Look for apps that tell you what they do with your data and how they keep it secure. Keep in mind that there is no legal limit on your liability with money stored in a shopping app (or on a gift card). Unless otherwise stated under the terms of service, you are responsible for all charges made through your shopping app.

Check your statements

Keep a record of your purchases and copies of confirmation pages, and compare them to your bank statements. If there is a discrepancy, report it immediately. (See Preventing and Responding to Identity Theft.)

Check privacy policies

Before providing personal or financial information, check the website's privacy policy. Make sure you understand how your information will be stored and used. (See Protecting Your Privacy.)

Understanding Your Computer: Web Browsers

Let's take a minute to talk about better understanding Your Computer, specifically Web Browsers.

Web browsers allow you to navigate the internet.

There are a variety of options available, so you can choose the one that best suits your needs.

How do web browsers work?

A web browser is an application that finds and displays web pages.

It coordinates communication between your computer and the web server where a particular website "lives."

When you open your browser and type in a web address or "URL" for a website, the browser submits a request to the server, or servers, that provide the content for that page.

The browser then processes the code from the server which is written in a language such as HTML, JavaScript, or XML.

Then it loads any other elements such as Flash, Java, or ActiveX that are necessary to generate content for the page.

After the browser has gathered and processed all of the components, it displays the complete, formatted web page.

Every time you perform an action on the page, such as clicking buttons and following links, the browser continues the process of requesting, processing, and presenting content.

How many browsers are there?

There are many different browsers.

Most users are familiar with graphical browsers, which display both text and graphics and may also display multimedia elements such as sound or video clips.

However, there are also text-based browsers. The following are some well-known browsers:

- Internet Explorer
- Firefox
- AOL
- Opera
- Safari - a browser specifically designed for Mac computers

- Lynx - a text-based browser desirable for vision-impaired users because of the availability of special devices that read the text

How do you choose a browser?

A browser is usually included with the installation of your operating system, but you are not restricted to that choice.

Some of the factors to consider when deciding which browser best suits your needs include

Compatibility.

Does the browser work with your operating system?

Security.

Do you feel that your browser offers you the level of security you want?

Ease of use.

Are the menus and options easy to understand and use?

Functionality.

Does the browser interpret web content correctly?

If you need to install other plug-ins or devices to translate certain types of content, do they work?

Appeal.

Do you find the interface and way the browser interprets web content visually appealing?

Can you have more than one browser installed at the same time?

If you decide to change your browser or add another one, you don't have to uninstall the browser that's currently on your computer.

You can have more than one browser on your computer at once.

However, you will be prompted to choose one as your default browser.

Anytime you follow a link in an email message or document, or you double-click a shortcut to a web page on your desktop, the page will open using your default browser.

You can manually open the page in another browser.

Most vendors give you the option to download their browsers directly from their websites.

Make sure to verify the authenticity of the site before downloading any files.

To further minimize risk, follow other good security practices, like using a firewall and keeping anti-virus software up to date.

Now you know the basics about web browsers, and better understand your computer.

Understanding Website Certificates

You may have been exposed to website, or host, certificates if you have ever clicked on the padlock in your browser or, when visiting a website, have been presented with a dialog box claiming that there is an error with the name or date on the certificate. Understanding what these certificates are may help you protect your privacy.

What are website certificates?

If an organization wants to have a secure website that uses encryption, it needs to obtain a site, or host, certificate. There are two elements that indicate that a site uses encryption (see Protecting Your Privacy for more information):

- a closed padlock, which, depending on your browser, may be located in the status bar at the bottom of your browser window or at the top of the browser window between the address and search fields
- a URL that begins with "https:" rather than "http:"

By making sure a website encrypts your information and has a valid certificate, you can help protect yourself against attackers who create malicious sites to gather your information.

You want to make sure you know where your information is going before you submit anything (see

Avoiding Social Engineering and Phishing Attacks for more information).

If a website has a valid certificate, it means that a certificate authority has taken steps to verify that the web address actually belongs to that organization. When you type a URL or follow a link to a secure website, your browser will check the certificate for the following characteristics:

1.   the website address matches the address on the certificate
2.   the certificate is signed by a certificate authority that the browser recognizes as a "trusted" authority

If the browser senses a problem, it may present you with a dialog box that claims that there is an error with the site certificate. This may happen if the name the certificate is registered to does not match the site name, if you have chosen not to trust the company who issued the certificate, or if the certificate has expired.

You will usually be presented with the option to examine the certificate, after which you can accept the certificate forever, accept it only for that particular visit, or choose not to accept it.

The confusion is sometimes easy to resolve (perhaps the certificate was issued to a particular department within the organization rather than the name on file). If you are unsure whether the certificate is valid or question the security of the site, do not submit personal information.

Even if the information is encrypted, make sure to read the organization's privacy policy first so that you know what is being done with that information (see Protecting Your Privacy for more information).

Can you trust a certificate?

The level of trust you put in a certificate is connected to how much you trust the organization and the certificate authority. If the web address matches the address on the certificate, the certificate is signed by a trusted certificate authority, and the date is valid, you can be more confident that the site you want to visit is actually the site that you are visiting.

However, unless you personally verify that certificate's unique fingerprint by calling the organization directly, there is no way to be absolutely sure.

When you trust a certificate, you are essentially trusting the certificate authority to verify the organization's identity for you. However, it is important to realize that certificate authorities vary in how strict they are about validating all of the information in the requests and about making sure that their data is secure.

By default, your browser contains a list of more than 100 trusted certificate authorities. That means that, by extension, you are trusting all of those certificate authorities to properly verify and validate the information. Before submitting any personal information, you may want to look at the certificate.

How do you check a certificate?

There are two ways to verify a web site's certificate in Internet Explorer or Firefox. One option is to click on the padlock icon. However, your browser settings may not be configured to display the status bar that contains the icon. Also, attackers may be able to create malicious websites that fake a padlock icon and display a false dialog window if you click that icon.

A more secure way to find information about the certificate is to look for the certificate feature in the menu options. This information may be under the file properties or the security option within the page information. You will get a dialog box with information about the certificate, including:

Who issued the certificate

You should make sure that the issuer is a legitimate, trusted certificate authority (you may see names like VeriSign, thawte, or Entrust). Some organizations also have their own certificate authorities that they use to issue certificates to internal sites such as intranets.

Who the certificate is issued to

The certificate should be issued to the organization who owns the website. Do not trust the certificate if the name on the certificate does not match the name of the organization or person you expect.

Expiration date

Most certificates are issued for one or two years. One exception is the certificate for the certificate authority itself, which, because of the amount of involvement necessary to distribute the information to all of the organizations who hold its certificates, may be ten years.

Be wary of organizations with certificates that are valid for longer than two years or with certificates that have expired.

Evaluating Your Web Browser's Security Settings

Check the security settings in your web browser to make sure they are at an appropriate level. While increasing your security may affect the functionality of some web sites, it could prevent you from being attacked.

Why are security settings for web browsers important?

Your web browser is your primary connection to the rest of the internet, and multiple applications may rely on your browser, or elements within your browser, to function. This makes the security settings within your browser even more important.

Many web applications try to enhance your browsing experience by enabling different types of functionality, but this functionality might be unnecessary and may leave you susceptible to being attacked.

The safest policy is to disable the majority of those features unless you decide they are necessary. If you determine that a site is trustworthy, you can choose to enable the functionality temporarily and then disable it once you are finished visiting the site.

Where can you find the settings?

Each web browser is different, so you may have to look around. For example, in Internet Explorer, you can find them by clicking **Tools** on your menu bar, selecting

Internet Options..., choosing the **Security** tab, and clicking the **Custom Level...** button.

However, in Firefox, you click **Tools** on the menu bar and select **Options....** Click the **Content**, **Privacy**, and **Security** tabs to explore the basic security options. Browsers have different security options and configurations, so familiarize yourself with the menu options, check the help feature, or refer to the vendor's web site.

While every application has settings that are selected by default, you may discover that your browser also has predefined security levels that you can select.

For example, Internet Explorer offers custom settings that allow you to select a particular level of security; features are enabled or disabled based on your selection.

Even with these guides, it is helpful to have an understanding of what the different terms mean so that you can evaluate the features to determine which settings are appropriate for you.

How do you know what your settings should be?

Ideally, you would set your security for the highest level possible. However, restricting certain features may limit some web pages from loading or functioning properly. The best approach is to adopt the highest level of security and only enable features when you require their functionality.

What do the different terms mean?

Different browsers use different terms, but here are some terms and options you may find:

• **Zones** - Your browser may give you the option of putting websites into different segments, or zones, and allow you to define different security restrictions for each zone.
For example, Internet Explorer identifies the following zones:
○ **Internet** - This is the general zone for all public web sites. When you browse the internet, the settings for this zone are automatically applied to the sites you visit. To give you the best protection as you browse,

---

you should set the security to the highest level; at the very least, you should maintain a medium level.

o **Local intranet** - If you are in an office setting that has its own intranet, this zone contains those internal pages. Because the web content is maintained on an internal web server, it is usually safe to have less restrictive settings for these pages. However, some viruses have tapped into this zone, so be aware of what sites are listed and what privileges they are being given.

o **Trusted sites** - If you believe that certain sites are designed with security in mind, and you feel that content from the site can be trusted not to contain malicious materials, you can add them to your trusted sites and apply settings accordingly. You may also require that only sites that implement Secure Sockets Layer (SSL) can be active in this zone. This permits you to verify that the site you are visiting is the site that it claims to be (see Protecting Your Privacy and Understanding Web Site Certificates for more information). This is an optional zone but may be useful if you personally maintain multiple web sites or if your organization has multiple sites. Even if you trust them, avoid applying low security levels to external sites—if they are attacked, you might also become a victim.

o **Restricted sites** - If there are particular sites you think might not be safe, you can identify them and define heightened security settings. Because the security settings may not be enough to protect you, the best precaution is to avoid navigating to any sites that make you question whether or not they're safe.

- **JavaScript** - Some web sites rely on web scripts such as JavaScript to achieve a certain appearance or functionality, but these scripts may be used in attacks (see Browsing Safely: Understanding Active Content and Cookies for more information).

- **Java and ActiveX controls** - These programs are used to develop or execute active content that provides some functionality, but they may put you at risk (see Browsing Safely: Understanding Active Content and Cookies for more information).

- **Plug-ins** - Sometimes browsers require the installation of additional software known as plug-ins to provide additional functionality. Like Java and ActiveX controls, plug-ins may be used in an attack, so before installing them, make sure that they are necessary and that the site you have to download them from is trustworthy.

You may also find options that allow you to take the following security measures:

- **Manage cookies** - You can disable, restrict, or allow cookies as appropriate. Generally, it is best to disable cookies and then enable them if you visit a site you trust that requires them (see Browsing Safely: Understanding Active Content and Cookies for more information).

• **Block pop-up windows** - Although turning this feature on could restrict the functionality of certain web sites, it will also minimize the number of pop-up ads you receive, some of which may be malicious (see Recognizing and Avoiding Spyware for more information).

Browsing Safely: Understanding Active Content and Cookies

Many people browse the Internet without much thought to what is happening behind the scenes.

Active content and cookies are common elements that may pose hidden risks when viewed in a browser or email client.

What is active content?

To increase functionality or add design embellishments, web sites often rely on scripts that execute programs within the web browser.

This active content can be used to create "splash pages" or options like drop-down menus.

Unfortunately, these scripts are often a way for attackers to download or execute malicious code on a user's computer.

JavaScript.

JavaScript is just one of many web scripts (other examples are VBScript, ECMAScript, and JScript) and is probably the most recognized.

Used on almost every web site now, JavaScript and other scripts are popular because users expect the functionality and "look" that it provides, and it's easy to incorporate.

Many common software programs for building web sites have the capability to add JavaScript features with little effort or knowledge required of the user.

However, because of these reasons, attackers can manipulate it to their own purposes.

A popular type of attack that relies on JavaScript involves redirecting users from a legitimate web site to a malicious one that may download viruses or collect personal information.

Java and ActiveX controls.

Different from JavaScript, Java and ActiveX controls are actual programs that reside on your computer or can be downloaded over the network into your browser.

If executed by attackers, untrustworthy ActiveX controls may be able to do anything on your computer that you can do such as running spyware and collecting personal information, connecting to other computers, and potentially doing other damage.

Java applets usually run in a more restricted environment, but if that environment isn't secure, then malicious Java applets may create opportunities for attack as well.

JavaScript and other forms of active content are not always dangerous, but they are common tools for attackers.

You can prevent active content from running in most browsers, but realize that the added security may limit functionality and break features of some sites you visit.

Before clicking on a link to a website that you are not familiar with or do not trust, take the precaution of disabling active content.

These same risks may also apply to the email program you use.

Many email clients use the same programs as web browsers to display HTML, so vulnerabilities that affect active content like JavaScript and ActiveX often apply to email. Viewing messages as plain text may resolve this problem.

What are cookies?

When you browse the Internet, information about your computer may be collected and stored.

This information might be general information about your computer such as IP address, the domain you used to connect like .edu, .com, and .net, and the type of browser you used.

It might also be more specific information about your browsing habits such as the last time you visited a particular web site or your personal preferences for viewing that site.

Cookies can be saved for varying lengths of time:

Session cookies.

Session cookies store information only as long as you're using the browser.

Once you close the browser, the information is erased.

The primary purpose of session cookies is to help with navigation, such as by indicating whether or not you've already visited a particular page and retaining information about your preferences once you've visited a page.

Persistent cookies.

Persistent cookies are stored on your computer so that your personal preferences can be retained.

In most browsers, you can adjust the length of time that persistent cookies are stored.

It is because of these cookies that your email address appears by default when you open your Yahoo! or Hotmail email account, or your personalized home page appears when you visit your favorite online merchant.

If an attacker gains access to your computer, he or she may be able to gather personal information about you through these files.

To increase your level of security, consider adjusting your privacy and security settings to block or limit cookies in your web browser. Read Evaluating Your Web Browser's Security Settings for more information.

To make sure that other sites are not collecting personal information about you without your knowledge, choose to only allow cookies for the web site you are visiting; block or limit cookies from a third-party.

If you are using a public computer, you should make sure that cookies are disabled to prevent other people from accessing or using your personal information.

Understanding Your Computer: Operating Systems

The operating system is the most fundamental program that runs on your computer.

It serves as the basis for how everything else works.

What is an operating system?

An operating system (OS) is the main program on a computer.

It performs a variety of functions, including:

Determining what types of software you can install

Coordinating the applications running on the computer at any given time

---

Making sure that individual pieces of hardware, such as printers, keyboards, and disk drives, all communicate properly

Allowing applications such as word processors, email clients, and web browsers to perform tasks on the system like drawing windows on the screen, opening files, communicating on a network and use other system resources like printers, and disk drives.

Reporting error messages

The OS also determines how you see information and perform tasks.

Most operating systems use a graphical user interface or GUI, which presents information through pictures including icons, buttons, and dialog boxes as well as words.

Some operating systems can rely more heavily on textual interfaces than others.

How do you choose an operating system?

In very simplistic terms, when you choose to buy a computer, you are usually also choosing an operating system.

Although you may change it, vendors typically ship computers with a particular operating system.

There are multiple operating systems, each with different features and benefits, but the following three are the most common:

Windows.

Windows, with versions including Windows XP, Windows Vista, and Windows 7, is the most common operating system for home users.

It's produced by Microsoft and is typically included on machines purchased in electronics stores or from vendors such as Dell or Gateway.

The Windows OS uses a GUI, which many users find more appealing and easier to use than text-based interfaces.

Mac OS X.

Produced by Apple, Mac OS X is the operating system used on Macintosh computers.

Although it uses a different GUI, it is conceptually similar to the Windows interface in the way it operates.

Linux and other UNIX-derived operating systems.

Linux and other systems derived from the UNIX operating system are frequently used for specialized workstations and servers, such as web and email servers.

Because they are often more difficult for general users or require specialized knowledge and skills to operate, they are less popular with home users than the other options.

However, as they continue to develop and become easier to use, they may become more popular on typical home user systems.

Understanding Internationalized Domain Names

You may have been exposed to internationalized domain names (IDNs) without realizing it. While they typically do not affect your browsing activity, IDNs may give attackers an opportunity to redirect you to a malicious web page.

What are internationalized domain names?

To decrease the amount of confusion surrounding different languages, there is a standard for domain names within web browsers.

Domain names are included in the URL (or web address) of a web site. This standard is based on the Roman alphabet (which is used by the English language), and computers convert the various letters into numerical equivalents.

This code is known as ASCII (American Standard Code for Information Interchange). However, other languages include characters that do not translate into this code, which is why internationalized domain names were introduced.

To compensate for languages that incorporate special characters (such as Spanish, French or German) or rely completely on character representation (such as Asian or Arabic languages), a new system had to be developed. In this new system, the base URL (which is usually the address for the home page) is dissected and converted into a format that is compatible with ASCII.

The resulting URL (which contains the string "xn--" as well as a combination of letters and numbers) will appear in your browser's status bar. In newer versions of many browsers, it will also appear in the address bar.

What are some security concerns?

Attackers may be able to take advantage of internationalized domain names to initiate phishing attacks (see Avoiding Social Engineering and Phishing Attacks for more information).

Because there are certain characters that may appear to be the same but have different ASCII codes (for example, the Cyrillic "a" and the Latin "a"), an attacker may be able to "spoof" a web page URL.

Instead of going to a legitimate site, you may be directed to a malicious site, which could look identical to the real one. If you submit personal or financial information while on the malicious site, the attacker could collect that information and then use and/or sell it.

How can you protect yourself?

Type a URL instead of following a link

Typing a URL into a browser rather than clicking a link within a web page or email message will minimize your risk. By doing this, you are more likely to visit the legitimate site rather than a malicious site that substitutes similar-looking characters.

Keep your browser up to date

Older versions of browsers made it easier for attackers to spoof URLs, but most newer browsers incorporate certain protections. Instead of displaying the URL that you "think" you are visiting, most browsers now display the converted URL with the "xn--" string.

Check your browser's status bar

If you move your mouse over a link on a web page, the status bar of your browser will usually display the URL that the link references. If you see a URL that has an unexpected domain name (such as one with the "xn--" string mentioned above), you have likely encountered an internationalized domain name.

If you were not expecting an internationalized domain name or know that the legitimate site should not need one, you may want to reconsider visiting the site.

Browsers such as Mozilla and Firefox include an option in their security settings about whether to allow the status bar text to be modified. To prevent attackers from taking advantage of JavaScript to make it appear that you are on a legitimate site, you may want to make sure this option is not enabled.

Evaluating Your Web Browser's Security Settings

Check the security settings in your web browser to make sure they are at an appropriate level. While increasing your security may affect the functionality of some web sites, it could prevent you from being attacked.

Why are security settings for web browsers important?

Your web browser is your primary connection to the rest of the internet, and multiple applications may rely on your browser, or elements within your browser, to function.

This makes the security settings within your browser even more important. Many web applications try to enhance your browsing experience by enabling different types of functionality, but this functionality might be unnecessary and may leave you susceptible to being attacked.

The safest policy is to disable the majority of those features unless you decide they are necessary.

If you determine that a site is trustworthy, you can choose to enable the functionality temporarily and then disable it once you are finished visiting the site.

Where can you find the settings?

Each web browser is different, so you may have to look around.

For example, in Internet Explorer, you can find them by clicking **Tools** on your menu bar, selecting **Internet Options**..., choosing the **Security** tab, and clicking the **Custom Level**... button.

However, in Firefox, you click **Tools** on the menu bar and select **Options**.... Click the **Content**, **Privacy, and Security** tabs to explore the basic security options.

Browsers have different security options and configurations, so familiarize yourself with the menu options, check the help feature, or refer to the vendor's web site.

While every application has settings that are selected by default, you may discover that your browser also has predefined security levels that you can select.

For example, Internet Explorer offers custom settings that allow you to select a particular level of security; features are enabled or disabled based on your selection.

Even with these guides, it is helpful to have an understanding of what the different terms mean so that you can evaluate the features to determine which settings are appropriate for you.

How do you know what your settings should be?

Ideally, you would set your security for the highest level possible.

However, restricting certain features may limit some web pages from loading or functioning properly.

The best approach is to adopt the highest level of security and only enable features when you require their functionality.

What do the different terms mean?

Different browsers use different terms, but here are some terms and options you may find:

Zones

Your browser may give you the option of putting websites into different segments, or zones, and allow you to define different security restrictions for each zone.
For example, Internet Explorer identifies the following zones:

Internet

This is the general zone for all public web sites. When you browse the internet, the settings for this zone are automatically applied to the sites you visit. To give you the best protection as you browse, you should set the security to the highest level; at the very least, you should maintain a medium level.

Local intranet

If you are in an office setting that has its own intranet, this zone contains those internal pages. Because the web content is maintained on an internal web server, it is usually safe to have less restrictive settings for these pages. However, some viruses have tapped into this zone, so be aware of what sites are listed and what privileges they are being given.

Trusted sites

If you believe that certain sites are designed with security in mind, and you feel that content from the site can be trusted not to contain malicious materials, you can add them to your trusted sites and apply settings accordingly.

You may also require that only sites that implement Secure Sockets Layer (SSL) can be active in this zone. This permits you to verify that the site you are visiting is the site that it claims to be (see Protecting Your Privacy and Understanding Web Site Certificates for more information).

This is an optional zone but may be useful if you personally maintain multiple web sites or if your organization has multiple sites. Even if you trust them, avoid applying low security levels to external sites—if they are attacked, you might also become a victim.

Restricted sites

If there are particular sites you think might not be safe, you can identify them and define heightened security settings. Because the security settings may not be enough to protect you, the best precaution is to avoid navigating to any sites that make you question whether or not they're safe.

JavaScript

Some web sites rely on web scripts such as JavaScript to achieve a certain appearance or functionality, but these scripts may be used in attacks (see Browsing Safely: Understanding Active Content and Cookies for more information).

Java and ActiveX controls

These programs are used to develop or execute active content that provides some functionality, but they may

---

put you at risk (see Browsing Safely: Understanding Active Content and Cookies for more information).

Plug-ins

Sometimes browsers require the installation of additional software known as plug-ins to provide additional functionality. Like Java and ActiveX controls, plug-ins may be used in an attack, so before installing them, make sure that they are necessary and that the site you have to download them from is trustworthy.

You may also find options that allow you to take the following security measures:

Manage cookies

You can disable, restrict, or allow cookies as appropriate. Generally, it is best to disable cookies and then enable them if you visit a site you trust that requires them (see Browsing Safely: Understanding Active Content and Cookies for more information).

Block pop-up windows

Although turning this feature on could restrict the functionality of certain web sites, it will also minimize the number of pop-up ads you receive, some of which may be malicious (see Recognizing and Avoiding Spyware for more information).

Defending Against Illicit Cryptocurrency Mining Activity

Malicious cyber actors use cryptocurrency-based malware campaigns to install crypto mining software and hijack the processing power of victim devices and systems to earn cryptocurrency.

However, there are steps users can take to protect their internet-connected systems and devices against this illicit activity.

The popularity of cryptocurrency, a form of digital currency, is rising.

Bitcoin, Litecoin, Monero, Ethereum, and Ripple are just a few types of the cryptocurrencies available.

Though cryptocurrency is a common topic of conversation, many people lack a basic understanding of cryptocurrency and the risks associated with it.

This lack of awareness is contributing to the rise of individuals and organizations falling victim to illicit cryptocurrency mining activity.

What is cryptocurrency?

Cryptocurrency is a digital currency used as a medium of exchange, similar to other currencies.

However, unlike other currencies, cryptocurrency operates independently of a central bank and uses encryption techniques and blockchain technology to secure and verify transactions.

What is crypto mining?

Cryptocurrency mining, or cryptomining, is simply the way in which cryptocurrency is earned.

Individuals mine cryptocurrency by using crypto mining software to solve complex mathematical problems involved in validating transactions.

Each solved equation verifies a transaction and earns a reward paid out in the cryptocurrency.

Solving cryptographic calculations to mine cryptocurrency requires a massive amount of processing power.

What is cryptojacking?

Cryptojacking occurs when malicious cyber actors exploit vulnerabilities that may be in web pages, software, and operating systems to illicitly install crypto mining software on victim devices and systems.

With the crypto mining software installed, the malicious cyber actors effectively hijack the processing power of the victim devices and systems to earn cryptocurrency.

Additionally, malicious cyber actors may infect a website with crypto mining JavaScript code, which leverages a visitor's processing power via their browser to mine cryptocurrency.

Cryptojacking may result in the following consequences to victim devices, systems, and networks:

Degraded system and network performance because bandwidth and central processing unit (CPU) resources are monopolized by crypto mining activity;

Increased power consumption, system crashes, and potential physical damage from component failure due to the extreme temperatures caused by cryptomining.

Disruption of regular operations;

Financial loss due to system downtime caused by component failure and the cost of restoring systems and files to full operation as well as the cost of the increased power consumption.

Cryptojacking involves maliciously installed programs that are persistent or non-persistent.

Non-persistent cryptojacking usually occurs only while a user is visiting a particular webpage or has an internet browser open.

Persistent cryptojacking continues to occur even after a user has stopped visiting the source that originally caused their system to perform mining activity.

Malicious actors distribute cryptojacking malware through weaponized mobile applications, botnets, and social media platforms by exploiting flaws in applications and servers, and by hijacking Wi-Fi hotspots.

What types of systems and devices are at risk for cryptojacking?

Any internet-connected device with a CPU is susceptible to cryptojacking.

The following are commonly targeted devices:

Computer systems and network devices

including those connected to information technology and Industrial Control System networks;

Mobile devices

devices are subject to the same vulnerabilities as computers; and

Internet of Things devices

internet-enabled devices such as printers, video cameras, and smart TVs.

How do you defend against cryptojacking?

The following cybersecurity best practices can help you protect your internet-connected systems and devices against cryptojacking:

Use and maintain antivirus software.

Antivirus software recognizes and protects a computer against malware, allowing the owner or operator to detect and remove a potentially unwanted program before it can do any damage. (See Understanding Anti-Virus Software.)

Keep software and operating systems up-to-date.

Install software updates so that attackers cannot take advantage of known problems or vulnerabilities. (See Understanding Patches.)

Use strong passwords.

Select passwords that will be difficult for attackers to guess, and use different passwords for different programs and devices. It is best to use long, strong passphrases or passwords that consist of at least 16 characters. (See Choosing and Protecting Passwords.)

Change default usernames and passwords.

Default usernames and passwords are readily available to malicious actors. Change default passwords, as soon as possible, to a sufficiently strong and unique password.

Check system privilege policies.

Review user accounts and verify that users with administrative rights have a need for those privileges.

Restrict general user accounts from performing administrative functions.

Apply application whitelisting.

Consider using application whitelists to prevent unknown executables from launching autonomously.

Be wary of downloading files from websites.

Avoid downloading files from untrusted websites. Look for an authentic website certificate when downloading files from a secure site. (See Understanding Web Site Certificates.)

Recognize normal CPU activity and monitor for abnormal activity.

Network administrators should continuously monitor systems and educate their employees to recognize any above-normal sustained CPU activity on computer workstations, mobile devices, and network servers. Any noticeable degradation in processing speed requires investigation.

Disable unnecessary services.

Review all running services and disable those that are unnecessary for operations. Disabling or blocking some services may create problems by obstructing access to files, data, or devices.

Uninstall unused software.

Review installed software applications and remove those not needed for operations. Many retail computer systems with preloaded operating systems come with toolbars, games, and adware installed, all of which can use excessive disk space and memory. These unnecessary applications can provide avenues for attackers to exploit a system.

Validate input.

Perform input validation on internet-facing web servers and web applications to mitigate injection attacks. On web browsers, disable JavaScript execution. For Microsoft Internet Explorer, enable the cross-site scripting filter.

Install a firewall.

Firewalls may be able to prevent some types of attack vectors by blocking malicious traffic before it can enter a computer system, and by restricting unnecessary outbound communications. Some device operating systems include a firewall. Enable and properly configure the firewall as specified in the device or system owner's manual. (See Understanding Firewalls.)

Create and monitor blacklists.

Monitor industry reports of websites that are hosting, distributing, and being used for malware command and control. Block the internet protocol addresses of known malicious sites to prevent devices from being able to access them.

INSPIRED? READY TO TAKE ACTION AND IMPLEMENT?

It's time to build your security culture anytime, anywhere, on any device. Not only do you get the tools and systems to become one of the most well-defended managed service providers around, you learn the

---

mindset it takes to become successful in cybersecurity and can pass both on to your clients.

You'll also learn more about how you can assess, educate, and monitor your staff. There are hundreds of ways to improve your security based on your unique business. Now is the time to become competition and recession-proof.

Visit www.HailBytes.com for free security resources!

Mobile Devices & Traveling

Keep safety standards in place when data is en route.

Savvy businesses understand the importance of securing sensitive information when it's outside the office. In Accretive, for example, the FTC alleged that an employee left a laptop containing more than 600 files, with 20 million pieces of information related to 23,000 patients, in the locked passenger compartment of a car, which was then stolen. The CBR Systems case concerned alleged unencrypted backup tapes, a laptop, and an external hard drive - all of which contained sensitive information - that were lifted from an employee's car. In each case, the business could have reduced the risk to consumers personal information by implementing reasonable security policies when data is en route. For example,When sending files, drives, disks, etc., use a mailing method that lets you track where the package is. Limit the instances when employees need to be out and about with sensitive data in their possession. But when there's a legitimate business need to travel with confidential information, employees should keep it out of sight and under lock and key whenever possible.

Protecting Your Portable Device: Physical Security

Many computer users, especially those who travel for business, rely on laptops and personal internet-enabled devices like smartphones and tablets because they are small and easily transported.

But while these characteristics make them popular and convenient, they also make them an ideal target for thieves.

Make sure to secure your mobile devices to protect both the machine and the information they contain.

What is at risk?

Only you can determine what is actually at risk. If a thief steals your laptop or mobile device, the most obvious loss is the machine itself.

However, if the thief is able to access the information on the computer or mobile device, all of the information stored on the device is at risk, as well as any additional information that could be accessed as a result of the data stored on the device itself.

Sensitive corporate information or customer account information should not be accessed by unauthorized people. You've probably heard news stories about organizations panicking because laptops with confidential information on them have been lost or stolen.

But even if there isn't any sensitive corporate information on your laptop or mobile device, think of the other information at risk: information about appointments, passwords, email addresses and other contact information, personal information for online accounts, etc.

How can you protect your laptop or internet-enabled device?

Password-protect your computer

Make sure that you have to enter a password to log in to your computer or mobile device (see Choosing and Protecting Passwords for more information).

Keep your valuables with you at all times

When traveling, keep your device with you. Meal times are optimum times for thieves to check hotel rooms for unattended laptops. If you are attending a conference or trade show, be especially wary—these venues offer thieves a wider selection of devices that are likely to contain sensitive information, and the conference sessions offer more opportunities for thieves to access guest rooms.

Downplay your laptop or mobile device

There is no need to advertise to thieves that you have a laptop or mobile device. Avoid using your device in public areas, and consider non-traditional bags for carrying your laptop.

Be aware of your surroundings

If you do use your laptop or mobile device in a public area, pay attention to people around you. Take precautions to shield yourself from "shoulder surfers"—make sure that no one can see you type your passwords or see any sensitive information on your screen.

Consider an alarm or lock

Many companies sell alarms or locks that you can use to protect or secure your laptop. If you travel often or will be in a heavily populated area, you may want to consider investing in an alarm for your laptop bag or a lock to secure your laptop to a piece of furniture.

Back up your files

If your mobile device is stolen, it's bad enough that someone else may be able to access your information.

To avoid losing all of the information, make backups of important information and store the backups in a separate location (see Good Security Habits for more information).

Not only will you still be able to access the information, but you'll be able to identify and report exactly what information is at risk.

What can you do if your laptop or mobile device is lost or stolen?

Report the loss or theft to the appropriate authorities. These parties may include representatives from law enforcement agencies, as well as hotel or conference staff. If your device contained sensitive corporate or customer account information, immediately report the loss or theft to your organization so that they can act quickly.

Protecting Your Portable Device: Data Security

Put Sensible Access Limits in Place.

Not everyone who might occasionally need to get on your networks should have an all-access, backstage pass. That's why it's wise to limit access to what's needed to get the job done. In the Dave & Buster's case, for example, the FTC charged that the company failed to adequately restrict third-party access to its network. By exploiting security weaknesses in the third-party company's system, an intruder allegedly connected to the network numerous times and intercepted personal information. What could the company have done to reduce that risk? It could have placed limits on third-party access to it's network - for example, by restricting connections to specified IP addresses or granting temporary, limited access.

In addition to taking precautions to protect your portable devices, it is important to add another layer of security by protecting the data itself.

Why do you need another layer of protection?

Although there are ways to physically protect your laptop, PDA, or other portable device (see Protecting Portable Devices: Physical Security for more information), there is no guarantee that it won't be stolen. After all, as the name suggests, portable devices are designed to be easily transported.

The theft itself is, at the very least, frustrating, inconvenient, and unnerving, but the exposure of information on the device could have serious consequences. Also, remember that any devices that are connected to the internet, especially if it is a wireless connection, are also susceptible to network attacks (see Securing Wireless Networks for more information).

What can you do?

Use passwords correctly

In the process of getting to the information on your portable device, you probably encounter multiple prompts for passwords. Take advantage of this security.

Don't choose options that allow your computer to remember passwords, don't choose passwords that thieves could easily guess, use different passwords for different programs, and take advantage of additional authentication methods (see Choosing and Protecting

Passwords and Supplementing Passwords for more information).

Consider storing important data separately

There are many forms of storage media, including CDs, DVDs, and removable flash drives (also known as USB drives or thumb drives). By saving your data on removable media and keeping it in a different location (e.g., in your suitcase instead of your laptop bag), you can protect your data even if your laptop is stolen.

You should make sure to secure the location where you keep your data to prevent easy access. It may be helpful to carry storage media with other valuables that you keep with you at all times and that you naturally protect, such as a wallet or keys.

Encrypt files

By encrypting files, you ensure that unauthorized people can't view data even if they can physically access it. You may also want to consider options for full disk encryption, which prevents a thief from even starting your laptop without a passphrase.

When you use encryption, it is important to remember your passwords and passphrases; if you forget or lose them, you may lose your data.

Install and maintain anti-virus software

Protect laptops and PDAs from viruses the same way you protect your desktop computer. Make sure to keep your virus definitions up to date (see Understanding Anti-Virus Software for more information).

If your anti-virus software doesn't include anti-spyware software, consider installing separate software to protect against that threat (see Recognizing and Avoiding Spyware and Coordinating Virus and Spyware Defense for more information).

Install and maintain a firewall

While always important for restricting traffic coming into and leaving your computer, firewalls are especially important if you are traveling and using different networks. Firewalls can help prevent outsiders from gaining unwanted access (see Understanding Firewalls for more information).

Back up your data

Make sure to back up any data you have on your computer onto a CD-ROM, DVD-ROM, or network (see Good Security Habits and Real-World Warnings Keep You Safe Online for more information). Not only will this ensure that you will still have access to the information if your device is stolen, but it could help you identify exactly which information a thief may be able to access.

You may be able to take measures to reduce the amount of damage that exposure could cause.

Holiday Traveling with Internet-Enabled Devices

The internet is at our fingertips with the widespread use of internet-enabled devices such as smartphones and tablets.

When traveling and shopping anytime, and especially during the holidays, consider the wireless network you are using when you complete transactions on your device.

Know the risks

Your smartphone, tablet, or other device is a full-fledged computer. It is susceptible to risks inherent in online transactions. When shopping, banking, or sharing personal information online, take the same precautions with your smartphone or other device that you do with your personal computer — and then some.

The mobile nature of these devices means that you should also take precautions for the physical security of your device (see Protecting Portable Devices: Physical Security for more information) and consider the way you are accessing the internet.

Do not use public Wi-Fi networks

Avoid using open Wi-Fi networks to conduct personal business, bank, or shop online. Open Wi-Fi networks at places such as airports, coffee shops, and other public locations present an opportunity for attackers to intercept sensitive information that you would provide to complete an online transaction.

If you simply must check your bank balance or make an online purchase while you are traveling, turn off your device's Wi-Fi connection and use your mobile device's cellular data internet connection instead of making the transaction over an unsecure Wi-Fi network.

Turn off Bluetooth when not in use

Bluetooth-enabled accessories can be helpful, such as earpieces for hands-free talking and external keyboards for ease of typing. When these devices are not in use, turn off the Bluetooth setting on your phone.

Cyber criminals have the capability to pair with your phone's open Bluetooth connection when you are not using it and steal personal information.

Be cautious when charging

Avoid connecting your mobile device to any computer or charging station that you do not control, such as a charging station at an airport terminal or a shared computer at a library.

Connecting a mobile device to a computer using a USB cable can allow software running on that computer to interact with the phone in ways that a user may not anticipate. As a result, a malicious computer could gain access to your sensitive data or install new software.

Don't fall victim to phishing scams

If you are in the shopping mode, an email that appears to be from a legitimate retailer might be difficult to resist. If the deal looks too good to be true, or the link in the email or attachment to the text seems suspicious, do not click on it!

What to do if your accounts are compromised

If you notice that one of your online accounts has been hacked, call the bank, store, or credit card company that owns your account. Reporting fraud in a timely manner helps minimize the impact and lessens your personal liability.

You should also change your account passwords for any online services associated with your mobile device using a different computer that you control. If you are the victim of identity theft, additional information is available from https://www.idtheft.gov/.

For even more information about keeping your devices safe, read Cybersecurity for Electronic Devices.

Privacy and Mobile Device Apps

Verify that privacy and security features work.

If your business offers software with a privacy or security feature, verify that the feature works as advertised. In TRENDnet, for example, the FTC charged that the company failed to test that an option to make a consumer's camera feed private would , in fact, restrict access to that feed. As a result, hundreds of "private" camera feeds were publicly available.

Similarly, in Snapchat, the company advertised that messages would "Disappear forever," but the FTC says it failed to ensure the accuracy of that claim. Among other things, the app saved video files to a location outside of the app's sandbox, making it easy to recover the video files with common file browsing tools. THe lesson for other companies: When offering privacy and security features, ensure that your product lives up to your advertising claims.

Mobile apps may gather information from your mobile device for legitimate purposes, but these tools may also put your privacy at risk.

Protect your data by being smart with the apps you install and reviewing the permissions each app has.

What are the risks associated with mobile device apps?

Applications (apps) on your smartphone or other mobile devices can be convenient tools to access the news, get directions, pick up a ride share, or play games. But these tools can also put your privacy at risk.

When you download an app, it may ask for permission to access personal information—such as email contacts, calendar inputs, call logs, and location data—from your device. Apps may gather this information for legitimate purposes—for example, a ride-share app will need your location data in order to pick you up.

However, you should be aware that app developers will have access to this information and may share it with third parties, such as companies who develop targeted ads based on your location and interests.

How can you avoid malicious apps and limit the information apps collect about you?

Before installing an app

Avoid potentially harmful apps (PHAs)

Reduce the risk of downloading PHAs by limiting your download sources to official app stores, such as your device's manufacturer or operating system app store. Do not download from unknown sources or install untrusted enterprise certificates.

Additionally—because malicious apps have been known to slip through the security of even reputable app stores—always read the reviews and research the developer before downloading and installing an app.

Be savvy with your apps

Before downloading an app, make sure you understand what information the app will access. Read the permissions the app is requesting and determine

---

whether the data it is asking to access is related to the purpose of the app.

Read the app's privacy policy to see if, or how, your data will be shared. Consider foregoing the app if the policy is vague regarding with whom it shares your data or if the permissions request seems excessive.

On already installed apps

Review app permissions

Review the permissions each app has. Ensure your installed apps only have access to the information they need, and remove unnecessary permissions from each app. Consider removing apps with excessive permissions. Pay special attention to apps that have access to your contact list, camera, storage, location, and microphone.

Limit location permissions

Some apps have access to the mobile device's location services and thus have access to the user's approximate physical location. For apps that require access to location data to function, consider limiting this access to when the app is in use only.

Keep app software up to date

Apps with out-of-date software may be at risk of exploitation of known vulnerabilities. Protect your mobile device from malware by installing app updates as they are released.

Delete apps you do not need

To avoid unnecessary data collection, uninstall apps you no longer use.

Be cautious with signing into apps with social network accounts

Some apps are integrated with social network sites—in these cases, the app can collect information from your social network account and vice versa. Ensure you are comfortable with this type of information sharing before you sign into an app via your social network account. Alternatively, use your email address and a unique password to sign in.

Visit www.HailBytes.com for free cybersecurity resources!

What additional steps can you take to secure data on your mobile devices?

Limit activities on public Wi-Fi networks

Public Wi-Fi networks at places such as airports and coffee shops present an opportunity for attackers to intercept sensitive information. When using a public or unsecured wireless connection, avoid using apps and websites that require personal information, e.g., a username and password. Additionally, turn off the Bluetooth setting on your devices when not in use. (See Cybersecurity for Electronic Devices.)

Be cautious when charging

Avoid connecting your smartphone to any computer or charging station that you do not control, such as a charging station at an airport terminal or a shared computer at a library. Connecting a mobile device to a computer using a USB cable can allow software running on that computer to interact with the phone in ways you may not anticipate. For example, a malicious computer could gain access to your sensitive data or install new software. (See Holiday Traveling with Personal Internet-Enabled Devices.)

Protect your device from theft

Having physical access to a device makes it easier for an attacker to extract or corrupt information. Do not leave your device unattended in public or in easily accessible areas. (See Protecting Portable Devices: Physical Security.)

Protect your data if your device is stolen

Ensure your device requires a password or biometric identifier to access it, so if it is stolen, thieves will have limited access to its data. (See Choosing and Protecting Passwords.) If your device is stolen, immediately contact your service provider to protect your data. (See the Federal Communications Commission's Consumer Guide: Protect Your Smart Device.)

INSPIRED? READY TO TAKE ACTION AND IMPLEMENT?

It's time to build your security culture anytime, anywhere, on any device. Not only do you get the tools and systems to become one of the most well-defended managed service providers around, you learn the mindset it takes to become successful in cybersecurity and can pass both on to your clients.

You'll also learn more about how you can assess, educate, and monitor your staff. There are hundreds of ways to improve your security based on your unique business. Now is the time to become competition and recession-proof.

Visit www.HailBytes.com for free security resources!

Congratulations!

You made it all the way to the end of the cybersecurity survival guide.

Remember, If you see something say something.

Here are a few indicators that something might be wrong.

Your computer may unexpectedly crash without clear reasons.

New files or programs with strange names will mysteriously appear.

They'll be sudden high system activity like your hard drive or your processor.

You'll see bizarre changes in filings or modification dates on your files.

There'll be a denial of service to whatever system or application you're trying to use.

You'll have unexplained poor system performance or you'll receive suspicious communication from unknown sources.

Now a little caveat here, just because you don't have access to the Internet or your system is slower than usual, doesn't necessarily mean you've been compromised or that you're experiencing a denial of service attack.

The best thing to do here is to reach out to your IT department and give them a heads up on the changes that you've noticed.

Strange system performance is one thing but if you do believe that you've been a victim of a phishing attack or some type of infection, immediately report the incident to your IT helpdesk or your security office.

The more information you can give them, like what you were doing around the time that you noticed things were different the better they can assist you.

If you're a home user, live in the United States, or you think or know that your identity has been compromised, use the Federal Trade Commission's resource at identitytheft.gov to report the incident and get guidance on your recovery plan.

If you believe that you might have revealed sensitive information about your organization even by accident and especially by accident, please report it to the appropriate people within your organization, including network administrators.

This can help your organization be on alert for any type of suspicious communications or unusual activity.

Thank you so much for joining me.

If I can explain something better or add something that you think is important please let me know.

I'm more than happy to keep this book updated in order to serve you.

Please leave an honest review on Amazon, as this does help me get more eyes on the book.

Other than that please have a great day and be safe out there.

Thank you for joining me on this journey.

Your Security Bonuses

As a thank you for buying this book, you can email me at david@hailbytes.com to learn more about any of the following 9 security bonuses for readers:

- FREE Vendor Due Diligence Security Checklist
- FREE Cyber Security Framework Self-Assessment

- FREEPhishing Posters
- FREE Phishing Simulation Trial
- FREE Phishing Server Trial
- FREE Basic Security Awareness Training Platform Trial
- FREE Advanced Security Awareness Training Platform Trial
- FREE Gramm-Leach-Bliley Act Checklist
- FREE Cybersecurity Framework Consultation

What's Next?

INSPIRED? READY TO TAKE ACTION AND IMPLEMENT?

It's time to build your security culture anytime, anywhere, on any device. Not only do you get the tools and systems to become one of the most well-defended managed service providers around, you learn the mindset it takes to become successful in cybersecurity and can pass both on to your clients.

You'll also learn more about how you can assess, educate, and monitor your staff. There are hundreds of ways to improve your security based on your unique business. Now is the time to become competition and recession-proof.

Visit www.HailBytes.com for free security resources!

About David McHale

Originally from tiny Kent Island, Maryland, David was homeschooled, and couldn't afford to finish college but taught himself how to program and write video games when he was 14 to escape his small-town roots and become an entrepreneur, building software and training programs to help businesses develop a strong cybersecurity culture fast on any device, anytime, anywhere, and on demand.

For David, it's not all about the money - watching one of his clients fall prey to an $8,000 illicit cryptojacking attack and learning the stories of countless other cyber victims has driven his passionate pursuit of his mission for a safer world for business owners.

David McHale is a professional security consultant that's helped over 450,000 individuals and thousands of organizations learn how to defend themselves from increasingly crafty cyber criminals.

Some of the organizations that have depended on his help in recent years include the Department of Transportation, the Federal Aviation Administration, and the Department of the Interior.

It is becoming increasingly important for organizations to develop a culture that prioritizes cyber security.

The training and security implementation are no longer just IT or security team functions.

They are now functions for everyone.

David is here to help each and every one of us learn how to better protect ourselves, our families, and our businesses.

Reach him by email at david@hailbytes.com, or by phone at (833) 892-3596.

He lives in the woods of Laurel with his wife, Safiya, and two orphaned dependents, Boden and Kinzey.

He can be reached at his business website at www.hailbytes.com

You can also follow him on Twitter: @hailbytes

And you can find him Facebook too:
www.Facebook.com/HailBytes

Other Products and Programs by David McHale

Please visit your favorite ebook retailer to discover my other books!

To hear about new books, and even receive free copies, email me at david@hailbytes.com with the subject line 'Book Updates'.

Monthly Phishing Simulations

$10 per user per month

We provide phishing simulations for you. You sign up, your users get phishing emails every month, and then they're educated with a funny edutainment style video if they click one of our phishing links.

On-Demand Phishing Servers

$1.27 per server per hour

Want complete control? We hand you the reins to a fully-loaded enterprise-grade phishing server and you can send your own campaigns as often as you want.

Basic Security Awareness Training Platform

$5 per user per month

Gain access to our video-based security training platform to give your staff 12 monthly videos on critical cybersecurity topics and help build your cybersecurity culture.

Advanced Security Awareness Training Platform

$14 per user per month

Gain access to our video-based security training platform to supercharge your staff with 84 weekly videos on critical cybersecurity topics and help build your cybersecurity culture

Written Information Security Program - Digital + Hardcover, with Annual Reprints

$990 one-time fee, then $490 per year

Get the foundational documents you need for a strong cybersecurity culture, your personalized organizational guide for what to do in a variety of information security situations.

National Institute Of Standards and Technology Cyber Security Framework Audit

$3,990 one-time fee, $990 per year

Get a meticulous audit from a certified information security professional to determine what your most critical cybersecurity risks are and develop a strategy to tackle your most critical cybersecurity problems.

Written Information Security Policies - Digital + Hardcover, with Annual Reprints
$290 one-time fee, then $190 per year

Get the foundational policies you need for a strong cybersecurity culture, your personalized policies for how to respond in a variety of information security situations.

If you want to learn more about any of these products or programs, don't hesitate to email me at david@hailbytes.com

---

Book David McHale To Speak!

Book David McHale as your Keynote Speaker and You're Guaranteed to Make Your Event Inspirational, Motivational, Highly Entertaining and Unforgettable!

For almost a decade, David McHale has been educating, entertaining, motivating and inspiring business owners, entrepreneurs, experts, and consultants to build and grow their business's security culture with his assess, educate, and monitor strategies for small business cybersecurity.

His origin story includes his recent near-death brush with liver failure, growing up lower middle-class in a small town in Kent Island Maryland, severe ADHD and "meeting" a cybercriminal through an aggressive cryptocurrency scam that changed his life forever.

After successfully building and implementing numerous cybersecurity programs in companies as large as 70,000 employees, David can share relevant, actionable strategies that anyone can use - even if they're starting from scratch.

His unique style inspires, empowers and entertains audiences while giving them the tools and strategies they need and want to build and grow successful security cultures for their brands and businesses.

For more info and to book David for your next event, text "Booking" to +1 (443) 362-9016.

Looking for more information?

HailBytes (**hailbytes.com)** has numerous free resources on cybersecurity for your benefit.

About HailBytes

HailBytes works for small business owners to prevent fraudulent, deceptive, and unfair practices in the marketplace. HailBytes gives you and your business tools to understand and comply with the law. Regardless of the size of your organization or the industry you're in, knowing - and fulfilling - your compliance responsibilities is smart, sound business. Visit Hailbytes at hailbytes.com or email me via david@hailbytes.com

Your Opportunity to Learn

Small businesses can ask questions to security experts at HailBytes without fear of being charged. To comment, call toll-free at 833-535-8064 or go to hailbytes.com/common-cybersecurity-questons

www.ingramcontent.com/pod-product-compliance
Lightning Source LLC
Chambersburg PA
CBHW021348210526
45463CB00001B/17